Ugly Little Greens

Gourmet Dishes Crafted from Foraged Ingredients

Mia Wasilevich

Professional Chef and Founder of Transitional Gastronomy

PAGE STREET
PUBLISHING CO.

For *Pascal Baudar*, my partner in all things. I'm so glad we foraged each other among the many thorny weeds out there. You have truly been a mentor and peer, opening up many doors and windows into my kitchen and heart. Thank you for being a teacher of foraging and plant identification, an example of how to research, and my inspiration and taste tester along with Max and Muppy.

Special thanks to *Melissa Brown Bidermann*, one of the most talented artists I could possibly hope to know. She created the beautiful plateware for the book with such love. In addition to her beautiful art, she's contributed much more than I can say in terms of friendship.

PAGE STREET
PUBLISHING CO.

First published in 2017 by
Page Street Publishing Co.
27 Congress Street, Suite 105
Salem, MA 01970
www.pagestreetpublishing.com

Distributed by Macmillan, sales in Canada by The Canadian Manda Group.

20 19 18 17   1 2 3 4

ISBN-13: 978-1-62414-387-8
ISBN-10: 1-62414-387-3

Library of Congress Control Number: 2016915231

Cover and book design by Page Street Publishing Co.
Photography by Mia Wasilevich except page 155 by Tiara Chiaramonte

Printed and bound in China

Page Street is proud to be a member of 1% for the Planet. Members donate one percent of their sales to one or more of the over 1,500 environmental and sustainability charities across the globe who participate in this program.

Contents

Chapter One

The Weeds in My Backyard and Beyond

Introduction – Why This Book About These Greens?

Being home, in every sense of the word, means that you recognize something intrinsically familiar, secure and comforting. For most people, me included, food is often the hub and intersection of these three things. In addition, we all crave authenticity in the foods we like to eat and cook and integrity in how we source them. I think most people who are a little food obsessed think this way, at least a little bit.

The "ugly little greens" I write about in this book represent that "home" or grounding source for me for a few reasons: they can be found almost everywhere and are welcomed in so many regions and countries throughout the world as a staple.

This book focuses on the greens that are most prevalent throughout North America and, largely, Canada. They are the everyday greens and unsung heroes that faithfully pop up year after year. They are not the regional or exotic finds; rather, they are the "salt of the earth" staples. The recipes contained here are a mixture of my everyday and entertaining repertoire. These are the kinds of recipes I make for friends as well as for simple home-cooked dinners. They are a combination of my travels, daily life experiences and what I find on the trails in my immediate environment. I can be home anywhere I find these plants.

My partner introduced me to the world of foraging almost a decade ago. As I learned about the plants in my area, I noticed that many of these plants (or ones very similar) were common, everyday foods in many of the countries I had visited as a child. Only here in North America, many people pay other people to weed them out of their yards. And there's no judgment from me—it's just that people have forgotten about these kinds of plants and mainly just don't know what to do with them. If I had a dime for every time someone has asked me what to do with the weeds in their garden . . . So I am writing a book about it.

In addition, in other parts of the world, people don't celebrate foraging in the same way we glamorize it here. (We can stop doing that now, I think.) It's just a part of the everyday way people do things in many other countries and in some parts of North America. I traveled a lot during my childhood, and those hyper-localized ingredients made the foods of various locales unique, special and memorable to me.

Once I reached adulthood and a short while after my partner introduced me to wild plants, I couldn't think of a reason not to use them as food as long as it was sustainable. I came to acknowledge that foraging is not only a practice in being self-reliant but also that these plants (and in particular the ones in this book) are both authentic to my environment and also universal, meaning they can grow in so many places all over the world and can be interpreted by so many cultures in so many different ways. I think that's neat.

If you take a little bit of time to research, you'll see and understand that foraging is not "new" by any means—there are people and groups who have been doing and teaching this for many, many years. I am but a respectful student and continuation of their knowledge and work.

Also, other plants that color my food experiences are the chaparral aromatics, like sages and fennel. I didn't include them in this book because they won't be available to most of you. In addition, I haven't included classics like nettle soup because there are many talented foragers who have included recipes like that in their books.

North, South, East and West I Go

I'd love to say that I spent many happy moments cooking in the kitchen with my grandmothers and mother, but that wouldn't be truthful. I'm not even sure any of them enjoyed cooking and, in retrospect, I can understand why. One grandmother had eleven children and the other thirteen and my mother just had to work a lot. Both grandmothers lived in poverty on opposite sides of the world, one an immigrant in a country so unlike her own and one native to a land that didn't want her there. I feel certain that they must have felt like the kitchen was an absolute burden. That never prevented our family from enjoying and appreciating food, though. And that's the magic of food. It knows no geographical, social or economic boundaries.

When I was growing up, my family decided to forgo the holiday season, not for any religious reasons, but because that's the only time anyone had off school or work. Although we were not wealthy and we came from a very modest middle class, my dad made it a priority to travel to world. We scrimped and saved to do this. So, from a very early age (around two or three years old), I boarded economy-class planes, boats and trains with my family every holiday season. And by the time I was twelve, I had traveled to more countries than most people do in a lifetime. I don't know how my parents did that with two small children, but I know I must have been such a little angel, right? I think they thought that we might not remember that toy or game in the years to come, but we would never forget the trip or experience. How right they were. It made me feel like an outsider to not have Christmas presents or a Christmas tree, but I can clearly see that this was the right thing for our family and I'm truly grateful.

While traveling, we gravitated away from the hotels and were attracted to the modest neighborhoods where many of the restaurants were mom-and-pop or tiny family-run places where they'd just invite you into the kitchen. I think that's just what my parents were used to and what they knew as opposed to the finest restaurants in the city (where I think they would have felt out of their league). I haven't been to most of those landmark restaurants you hear about but hopefully I will someday. In the meantime, I'm happy to hang out in the kitchen with everyday chefs who love their craft.

I'm convinced that frequenting humble mom-and-pop restaurants as a child is the reason I have such a deep connection to comfort food, country food, roadside food and traditional foods. I literally felt at home in every country I visited because someone's grandmother was cooking for me. In essence, I was studying the cooking practices, techniques and traditions of a whole lot of grandmas throughout my entire childhood, and because I didn't speak their language, we spoke through food.

I'm half Native American from the Southwest and half Russian by way of Argentina. That's a lot of food culture right there. This, coupled with the amount of traveling we did as kids and the boom of food TV, created a food wanderlust in me. I now live in Los Angeles, where I don't have to drive far to have an authentic ethnic food experience from just about anywhere in the world. I'm inspired by my travels, my neighbors and the neighborhoods I have lived in (Korean, Persian, Armenian and Salvadorian, just to name a few).

If I'm making something or have a recipe in this book that seems foreign or exotic, it isn't exotic to me or my experiences. There are some definite Asian preferences in my palate. That said, I am an absolute champion of American food. I'm in love with it and am proud of all the regional specialties we have. If I had to describe my personal culinary style, it would be American, despite all the international and family influences. To me, the real American food is a microcosm of all the people who live here and have lived here. I'd love for these weedy staples to become more a staple of American food, as they must've been years ago.

What Is This Book? What Can It Be for You?

This book is an excellent jumping-off point for someone who has done some study and research about wild and foraged edible plants already. I give you some tips on where to start with basic taxonomy and identification with images, where the plants fit within plant families, as well as some field guide and foraging resources in the back of the book. I hope to whet your curiosity to study even more deeply on your own with the recipes in this book. That's how I got into foraging and cooking with foraged ingredients. As I learned about foraging, my amazement grew that these weeds could be not just survival food but food that I craved, enjoyed gathering and loved cooking.

If you haven't researched wild edible plants before, this is an excellent place to start, as the plants in this book are among the most common and easily recognizable in North America (as well as in some other parts of the world). Essentially, they are common weeds that are native nuisances, introduced or a hybrid of both.

Books, online studies and apps are a wonderful introduction to studying edible and foraged plants. But because no one is an expert of everything, we need local experts who are dedicated as well. Nature is not general but adapts to each region, so your particular region or area will vary in plant species. I think by now there are a few plant ID apps as well. I would like to emphasize that, in addition to your diligent studies, an actual person teaching you is the best source for learning about the edible plants around you. I suggest connecting with a local group or expert in your area from time to time.

Why should you seek out local experts for advice? Foraging is very much an oral tradition passed from one person to another. I feel that the connection between two people—teacher-to-student, face-to-face—creates an awareness and sense of responsibility that can't always be duplicated from learning something online or from a book. Plus, the validation from an expert gives you added confidence in being able to identify your finds. Also, familiarizing yourself and becoming an expert on at least five plants, however common they are, will go a long way in teaching you to be detail-oriented and diligent about being able to positively identify a plant before you consume it.

I'm a cook. I've had no professional training other than studying it on my own, with mentors and applying my knowledge for the past decade in my work. We're all always learning. All I know is that I'm madly in love with the creative and artistic aspect of cooking. It makes me extremely happy to cook for my clients, family and friends and I've been doing that my whole life. This book is not filled with difficult cooking techniques and, for the most part, it has very simple, basic ingredients. I style them fancy sometimes, but the ingredients themselves are super basic.

I don't use complicated, specialized tools, and I often cook outdoors. The recipes in this book are mainly meant to be cooked on the stovetop and in the oven. The most specialized tools you'll need are a digital scale, high-speed food processor or immersion blender, a cream whipper, tongs, a good strainer, garden pruners, scissors and maybe some gardening gloves.

As far as my pantry, I always have a variety of flours (all-purpose, corn, rice, hazelnut, almond, arrowroot, potato, sorghum and tapioca, to name a few), legumes, whole grains, cooking wines and vinegars, homemade and store-bought. I have a good selection of dried herbs and spices, wild-crafted and from the garden and market. I also have a variety of fats to cook with, from coconut oil to duck fat, lard, olive oil, bacon fat and plenty of butter.

It's a little bit like a cooking competition show when you're working with foraged materials. You may have a vague idea of what's in season, but there's no guarantee of what you'll find, even in your own garden, and you just have to come up with something on the fly. A pantry stocked with a diverse flavor palette of fats, vinegars, wines, flours, legumes and herbs are what keep my ideas flowing.

This book is meant to inspire you to come up with different recipe ideas, techniques, takes or approaches with the "ugly little greens" you have in your life, whether they grow in the field or in your own yard. I wholeheartedly hope you change up the recipes, make additions and subtractions, or just check out the recipe and run in a completely different direction with the ideas presented in this book. I know that's what I do when I read cookbooks. They are a starting point. Be creative and taste everything, please!

Don't Take Grandmother: Responsible Harvesting

While the following may not be the sexiest reading material, it's really important to take it in. Even if you've heard this information before, it's an important reminder.

According to the United States Department of Agriculture (USDA), there are nine plant classifications. You can visit the USDA website to read more thorough definitions, but I've included the brief definitions that follow:

- Native—A plant that is a part of the balance of nature that has developed over hundreds or thousands of years in a particular region or ecosystem.

- Invasive—A plant that is both non-native and able to establish on many sites, grow quickly and spread to the point of disrupting plant communities or ecosystems.

- Naturalized—A non-native plant that does not need human help to reproduce and maintain itself over time in an area where it is not native.

- Exotic and Opportunistic—A native plant that is able to take advantage of disturbance to the soil or existing vegetation to spread quickly and out-compete the other plants on the disturbed site.

- Translocated—A plant not native to the continent on which it is now found.

- Weed—A plant (native or non-native) that is not valued in the place where it is growing.

- Noxious Weed—A plant that is particularly troublesome or any plant or plant product that can directly or indirectly injure or cause damage to crops (including nursery stock or plant products), livestock, poultry or other interests of agriculture, irrigation, navigation, the natural resources of the United States, the public health or the environment.

As you can see by these definitions, native plants hold a special place at the top of this list, because they are an integral part of our environment, ecosystem and, importantly, our very culture. Native plants are what make where you are unique and reflective of your *terroir*. They make up the colors, textures and smells that make it "home." I know that when I travel and return home, the smell of sages, chaparral brush and yerba santa welcome and embrace me. In addition, native plants are an integral and participatory part in our chain of survival. If you want to use native plants, learn how to plant or propagate them.

In addition to learning how to plant or propagate native plants, it's important that you "don't take Grandmother." What I mean by this is that there is a hierarchy in the plant world, especially when it comes to harvesting. You want to leave the oldest, largest and most established plants and take special care not to uproot them or disturb their growth. They likely have seeded the area around them, ensuring the species' survival.

As I learned more and nature became more a part of my everyday life, I saw that the term "forager" is an incomplete title. Many of the "foragers" I know (people who actually use the plants for food and medicine) are also self-reliance educators, food preservers, ethnobotanists, naturalists, permaculture instructors, native-plant gardeners, farmers and stewards of the environment.

People who actually forage for food as a daily means of subsistence and those who use foraged plants as food and medicine know all too well that it's not easy. It's hard work— very hard work. It's not like the supermarket, where you will always find apples where the apples always are and broccoli where the broccoli always is. Seeds and plants move around, wildfires and flooding happen, climates fluctuate.

For these reasons, many people who forage also participate in forming food gardens and permaculture groups, giving as much as they take and learning to replant responsibly. I don't think these are just options anymore. I know these are things I'm actively exploring as I learn more as well.

I came across this list of Honorable Harvesting Guidelines from Wolf Camp and the Conservation College in Puyallup, Washington. Many foragers, naturalists, wildcrafters, conservationists and ethnobotany groups have rules of foraging and harvesting, all of which offer sound and responsible advice and suggestions. I love this set of guidelines, because it is eloquent and to the point. I added number 10.

Honorable Harvesting Guidelines

1. Do you need it? Harvest with a purpose in mind, not just for the fun of it.

2. Harvest only as much as you will use and process it as soon as possible (don't waste it).

3. 1 in 20 rule. It's OK to harvest a plant if there are 20 others available to maintain the population.

4. Leave Grandmother. Allow the biggest and best plants to remain so they can continue to propagate the healthiest population.

5. Leave damaged plants or plants with "residents." Select quality material for your food and medicine. If a critter makes a home there, choose another.

6. Harvest ⅓ or less of an individual plant (leave some roots) so it can continue and thrive.

7. Avoid polluted areas.

8. Offer appreciation and bring positive energy to your harvest.

9. Never put anything in your mouth unless you are 100 percent sure it is safe to ingest.

10. Be cognizant of where you are foraging. Are you on public parkland? Are you on ancestral or native land? Be respectful of where you forage and if it's allowed or not. Always ask permission.

Lastly, there will be disagreement among various groups whether to forage and what to forage. What I would love to see is people talking to each other with respect and compassion and really communicating. More often than not, we have much more in common than we think. If we could be as mindful of each other as we are to the plants, we'd have something special, wouldn't we?

Taxonomy and Identification

First question: Where to start?

Well, being curious and reading a book on the subject is the first and most important step. So, you've accomplished that already!

Second question: How and where do you start looking for plants to harvest?

This is a little more difficult to answer, but I'll take you through my thought process and hopefully that will clear a few things up for you and get you on your way. Unfortunately, there are no maps that I know of that pinpoint exactly where things are growing with up-to-the-minute accuracy.

I would start by simply surveying your own yard or property and seeing what is actually already growing there, weeds and all. Chances are good that a few of the weeds featured in this book are growing right under your nose. Feel free to use this book and other field guides on the plant you are observing. Take the books with you as reference. When I first started, I carried more than a few books with me and sat in a field with my loupe for hours.

Third question: What is taxonomy?

Taxonomy is a scientific, orderly classification of plants and animals according to their presumed natural relationships or a scientific system that provides identification, classification and description. It's like a detailed checklist of the plants' components and characteristics that helps you confidently identify them. Even if I absolutely know what a plant is, I'll still practice this kind of detailed identification from time to time as it gets me into the habit of remembering what questions to ask when I encounter a plant I don't know.

Next, survey your local parks and nature preserves for identification purposes only. Do you see some similar plants? Good, great!

Now take some notes on a few things:

— What time of year is it? What's the weather like? This tells you what time of year the particular plant you are observing grows in your area and under what weather conditions.

— Where is this particular plant growing? On a shady hillside? Near water? In sandy soil? In bright sunlight? Under trees? Also, observe what plants and shoots pop up directly after rain. This tells you in what conditions the particular plant you are observing grows.

— Does this plant consistently grow by another plant? This will vary from area to area and region to region, but some things will remain fairly consistent. For example, if the plant is riparian, or needs to grow by a river or in a stream (e.g., watercress and cattail), that's most likely where you'll always find it.

— What does this plant look like at different stages in its growth? Knowing what the shoots, mature plant, flowers, stems and seeds look like throughout the plant's life cycle is so valuable and enlightening. Worth noting is that many shoots look nearly indistinguishable from each other when they are tiny and just coming out of the ground. When they are that small, I may not be able to tell one tiny dicot (a seed that branches off into two leaves when it sprouts as opposed to a monocot, which forms one small leaf when it sprouts out of the ground) from another without a microscope. Also, it's sometimes difficult to identify plants, when starting, without their flower. So again, knowing what the plant looks like in all of its life stages is key.

Most of the plants in this book will appear anywhere from late winter to midsummer depending on your climate. For example, I live in California, where it's warmer and drier than many other parts of the United States. So, I'm on the lookout for shoots and greens earlier in the year than the Midwest, North and East. I'll start to gather or harvest plants in late winter and usually finish in midspring as it starts to get hot and dry (unless we get some rain). If you live in the Northeast, however, you may get much more spring and summer rain and will be able to harvest later in the season.

In sum, being your own diligent student in addition to utilizing guidebooks, online resources and the tips offered here will serve you best in the long term and increase your confidence and, hopefully, curiosity.

In the pages that follow, I will highlight the family the plant comes from so you have a starting place to do research, what type of plant it is (e.g., native or invasive), the plant's flavor profile, a few main, distinguishing identifiers for each plant as a refresher and some common look-alikes to be aware of. Because this book focuses on greens, almost all of these plants are harvested from late winter to early summer.

A Note About Safe Foraging

It's important to mention that you need to be aware of the areas where you are foraging. Has the area been sprayed with chemicals? Is it near a polluted water runoff (e.g., an equestrian center or golf course)? Is it in an area where people walk their dogs? You, of course, want to make sure you are foraging in safe, nontoxic conditions and water sources.

How to Prep and Store Your Harvest

Note: Use breathable canvas bags or a basket when harvesting. You can place the plants inside and then pour some water over them to keep them hydrated, especially if it's hot out.

I must admit that the meticulous cleaning and storing of my forages is my least favorite part of harvesting plants. It's an important step, though, because if they are not cleaned or stored properly, they can either dry out or rot quickly and then you will have wasted them. It's a little tedious, but necessary. With the exception of elderflowers, I submerge and soak all harvested forages. I have a variety of food-grade buckets and small barrels. I can then reuse the water in the garden or on the trees.

Chickweed, Miner's Lettuce, Purslane, Chervil, Nasturtium, Oxalis, Nettles, Mallow and Lambsquarters

Shoots, tender leaves and herbs are the most delicate of foraged plants, and if I am harvesting, I want to get them into a sink or bucket full of cold, clean water as soon as possible.

I soak the more tender harvests for 20 minutes, gently agitating to loosen any dirt clumps, leaves and little critters (such as ladybugs, caterpillars and crickets). Take care to release any creatures back into the wild.

If I'm using the plants the same day and it's not hot, I will stand the plants upright, stems first, in water in a smaller container or bowl. This works out great for watercress, nasturtium and purslane, especially. If you are not using the plants right away, take care to shake the water off the plants thoroughly (or use a large salad spinner if you have one). Too much moisture and they'll rot very quickly. (There is nothing like the smell of rotting nettles—my goodness.) The way I get rid of the excess water is quite ridiculous, but effective. I'll place the plants (stems all facing one direction) in a large, clean kitchen towel, gather the corners of the towel, go outside and in a windmill fashion, vigorously swing the bundle by the corners. I must look insane—but hey, it works.

I then roll out five or six paper towels (still connected to each other), place the plants at one end and gently and loosely roll them like a jelly roll. Then I'll store them in jumbo zip-top bags and seal the bags three-quarters of the way. Don't crowd your refrigerator, because the plants need a bit of circulation.

I don't wash or rinse elderberry flowers. The beauty and fragrance is in the pollen. I do rinse and soak the berries. Acorns have their own procedure that we'll go into on page 206. I store or hang the acorns in a breathable cloth (such as a burlap sack or old pillow case) in a cool, dry place off the ground.

Watercress, Cattail Shoots and Curly Dock

Because these grow near or in water, I soak these longer and change the water once or twice. I want them not only to rehydrate but also to release anything they've soaked up. You want to forage only in clean water sources, of course, but I like to take this extra precaution. After washing and soaking, I remove the excess water and wrap the plants as I described earlier.

Note: Always pick plants 1 to 2 inches (3 to 6 cm) above the water level to avoid bacteria.

Chapter Two

Delightfully Delicate and Tender

Shoots, Leaves and Herbs

Chickweed, Miner's Lettuce, Milk Thistle, Watercress, Nasturtium, Oxalis

In the spring, at the end of the day, you should smell like dirt.

– Margaret Atwood, *Bluebeard's Egg*

Although there's no definitive way to describe the smell of sprouting spring and the fields, meadows, trails and hills, I would call it delicate. The new herbs and shoots taste like a cross between dew and baby lettuce, some more verdant, some lemony and some herbal. In spring, these plants are so tender, clean and fresh and can be eaten straight out of the ground. They are best paired with other clean and mild flavors. They brighten almost any dish.

Throughout the winter and spring, a variety of little greens shoot up that are the staples of a harvested salad. They seem to pop up overnight both in open fields and disturbed soils. Just as quickly, they disappear as the weather changes, so I'm almost always on the lookout for them. In our area, these little weeds all grow together, along with their toxic look-alikes. It's important to know the area you are harvesting from well to make an absolutely accurate assesment when identifying a plant.

Some years are better than others. At the time of this writing, we had hot and dry weather very early, so the foraging season for these types of plants was very short. Following are a few of the main "salad staples" that are commonly found in North America, along with a brief overview of each. As you'll notice, almost all of them are the plants so many people spend so much time trying to rid their yards or gardens of. We often have permanent permission to access our neighbors' properties. Some of them are starting to get curious enough to try them, though. Note: Do not take plants from someone's property without permission or if they spray herbicides in the area.

In general, I don't like to cook these kinds of plants. I prefer to eat them in their natural state, and I've given a few salad ideas in the book.

Chickweed

Stellaria media

Pink family (Caryophyllaceae)

Introduced from Europe; invasive

Flavor Profile

Chickweed's flavor is reminiscent of pea shoots or young corn shoots. It's very tender, but it holds up remarkably well in a salad dressing and doesn't wilt down immediately. Young chickweed has a pleasant, slightly sweet aftertaste.

When and How to Harvest

This plant likes cooler weather and starts popping up in early winter in fields and disturbed soils. In some areas, it can have up to three seasons. You will most likely find chickweed wherever there is disturbed or previously cultivated fertile soil. It likes a nice, moist, rich soil and does not like heat or extreme sunlight, so look to dappled, shaded fields or hillsides.

When I see a beautiful little carpet of chickweed, it makes me happy. I usually use a curved knife or sharp scissors and gently grab a handful of the leaves and cut the stems beneath while holding them securely. Cut the stems while in a gathered bunch as close to the leaves as possible. It's better to do this when you harvest as opposed to when you wash them as it will end up in a tangle that will be difficult to sort and trim.

Top: Chickweed (*Stellaria media*) leaves and stems and bottom: a toxic chickweed look-alike called spurge (*Chamaesye maculate*).

Mature chickweed (*Stellaria media*)

Also, very important, try to make it look like you were never there. Harvest in small patches and not all in one place.

Distinguishing Identifiers

- One line of hairs going down the stem

- Filament inside the stem when you break it

- Small white flowers with five petals (they look like ten petals, but they're actually five petals divided in two)

- Opposite, alternate leaves

Common Look-Alikes

- **Spurge** (*Chamaesye maculate*: extremely toxic, can cause death); has a milky sap

- Scarlet pimpernel (*Anagallis arvensis*); has brightly colored flowers

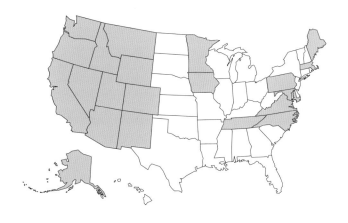

Current Known Range

Miner's Lettuce

Claytonia perfoliata
Miner's lettuce family (Montiaceae)
Native to North and Central America

Flavor Profile

The leaves are both juicy and velvety at the same time. It's succulent and delicate. Handle it sparingly as it gets crushed easily. To me, this is the most like lettuce in terms of flavor and reminds me of butter lettuce in texture. The leaves are mild throughout the plant's growth cycle and only slightly bitter as the weather gets warmer.

When and How to Harvest

In late winter to early spring, miner's lettuce springs up in almost any soil condition, from sandy and gravelly soil to rocky crags and rich peaty soil. In my area, I find it mostly on rocky, shady hillsides. It has a short season (maybe a few weeks), but it can reseed quickly, as well. To harvest, I use sharp scissors and snip the stalks just under the round leaves.

Miner's lettuce (*Claytonia perfolata*)

Distinguishing Identifiers

- Round leaves with center stem and flower

- Small white or pink flowers with five petals

Possible Look-Alikes

- None that I am aware of; there are regional subspecies that are slightly different, but they are very similar

Purslane

Portulaca oleracea

Portulacaceae family

Both native and introduced; invasive

Also called verdolaga, pigweed and moss rose, this used to include the miner's lettuce family but is now its own family with only one genus; it's considered an exotic or introduced weed and grows in almost every part of the world.

Flavor Profile

The leaves are succulent and juicy and at different times of the season, purslane has a slight salty flavor as it draws minerals from the earth. It's fairly delicate, so take a small bucket of water to store it in for the ride or hike home. It doesn't keep very well in paper towels or bags in the refrigerator. Keep it stem down in a bowl of cold water until use, changing the water frequently. The stems are just as delicious as the leaves and have a "pop" when you bite into them.

When and How to Harvest

Pretty much all this plant needs is sunlight. It can be found throughout summer in warmer weather. You might see this plant growing near an outdoor water spigot, water runoff or in moist soil, but it also thrives in drier soil as well and can adapt to most soil conditions. Harvest later in the day as the plant goes into a "sleep cycle" at night and converts carbon dioxide to malic acid and then converts it to glucose throughout the day. It's sweeter if collected in the afternoon as opposed to the morning.

Distinguishing Identifiers

- Succulent opposite leaves
- Reddish stems

Possible Look-Alikes

- Spurge (*Chamaesyce maculata*)

Bur Chervil

Anthriscus caucalis

Apiaceae family

Introduced from Europe; invasive

Caution: In our area, we find only bur chervil, but there are a few other species. I do not suggest using this herb until you can positively identify this plant with a thorough taxonomy and a foraging teacher or guide. It looks too similar to poison hemlock, especially when young.

Bur Chervil Range

Current Known Range

Flowering purslane (*Portulaca oleracea*)

Top: Bur chervil (*Anthriscus caucalis*) and bottom: poison hemlock (*Conium maculatum*)

Detail of the tiny hairs on the stems of bur chervil (*Anthriscus caucalis*)

Flavor Profile

A very delicate herbal flavor that is a combination of anise, cilantro and crushed carrot greens. It's much lighter and subtler in flavor than cilantro. The feathery leaves and beautiful tiny flowers are beautiful as a garnish but this herb can definitely flavor a dish.

When and How to Harvest

This herb grows prolifically and covers shady hillsides in early spring, but its season is really short (a month at most in my area). It loves shady, cool, rich, moist soil. The best place to look is shaded forest areas with deep hillsides and ravines. Use sharp scissors to snip. Don't discard the stems as they are also usable, especially in soup stocks.

Distinguishing Identifiers

- Feathery, triangular leaves
- Small white flowers
- Hollow stems
- Tiny hairs on stems
- Smells like chervil when crushed

Possible Look-Alikes

- **Poison hemlock** (*Conium maculatum*: extremely toxic, can cause death)
- Queen Anne's lace (*Daucus carota*)

Milk Thistle

Silybum marianum

Asteraceae family, Carduoideae or thistle subfamily

Introduced from southern Europe
and grows worldwide; invasive

Also called blessed milk thistle

Flavor Profile

The young leaves are edible and can be used raw or cooked.
(I prefer cooked.) The young stalks are sweet and crunchy and
remind me of a cross between celery and artichokes and are
very similar to cardoons in flavor, as well. I like the stems raw
or lightly tossed in warm butter or olive oil.

When and How to Harvest

You start to see the vivid purple flowers from early spring to
early summer in sandy, rocky soil. I harvest in early spring,
while the plants are still tender. This can be tricky to harvest
as it gets older; the stalks develop some prickly spines. Use
heavy garden gloves and a sharp knife to harvest the stalks.
Right before consuming, peel back the outer skin of the stalks,
much like you would when removing the strings from celery.
Inside, the stalk is tender, juicy and sweet. I will soak them for
10 to 15 minutes to remove any bitter aftertaste. They also
oxidize, so after you peel them, store them in acidulated water
until use or they will discolor.

Milk thistle (*Silybum marianum*)

Milk Thistle Range

Current Known Range

Distinguishing Identifiers

- Purple flower heads
- White-veined leaves
- Impressive height (the talks can get quite tall)

Possible Look-Alikes

- Bull thistle (*Cirsium vulgare*)

Watercress

Nasturtium officinale

Brassicaceae family (Cruciferae)

Introduced from Europe;
noxious and invasive in most
of the United States

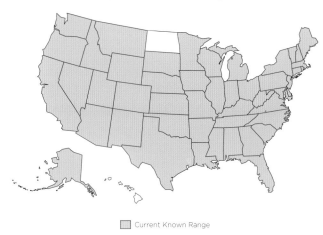

☐ Current Known Range

Flavor Profile

Spicy and bold. Opens up the nasal passages. The leaves, stems and flowers have a pleasant texture. Don't underestimate the use of the stems, especially in a crunchy salad or lightly sautéed as a vegetable alongside a steak.

When and How to Harvest

This typically starts to grow in early spring, but we see it growing throughout the summer as well. It's riparian and grows near or in water. Even if the water source is pristine, always collect the plants above the waterline using sharp pruners. The flowers, leaves and stems are all edible.

Distinguishing Identifiers

- Hollow stems
- Compound pinnate leaves
- White flowers
- Semiaquatic or aquatic

Possible Look-Alikes

- Fool's watercress (*Apium nodiflorum*)
- **Water hemlock** (*Cicuta maculata*: extremely toxic, can cause death)

Watercress field (*Nasturtium officinale*)

Nasturtium

Tropaeolum majus

Tropaeolaceae family

Introduced from Europe, native to Central and South America; invasive

Although this does not grow in the wild in every state, I've included it here because it's not uncommon to find this in someone's yard or garden, even if they didn't plant it. We see a lot of invasive nasturtium where we are.

Flavor Profile

Wasabi-like. Very spicy and pungent, like watercress (possibly even more so). It has a nice clean, green aftertaste that can be slightly sweet. The young leaves and stalks are tender. The flower buds and seeds are edible, as well.

When and How to Harvest

There are patches near my location that are easily a few acres. The plant can either climb hillsides or grow in clustering bunches in poor or rich soil. The best specimens are taken from shady or dappled areas. Nasturtium is best eaten fresh, so I take only what I need that day when it is in season, which is midspring to early summer.

Nasturtium Range

Current Known Range

Garden nasturtium (Tropaeolum majus) growing alongside Oxalis.

Distinguishing Identifiers

- Round, alternate hairless leaves (they look like lily pads)
- Showy, bright flowers (pastels, reds, oranges, yellows)
- Nut-like fruit

Possible Look-Alikes

- None that I know of that would grow near or around this plant

Oxalis

Oxalis L.

Oxalidaceae family

Both native and introduced; grows worldwide

Also called sour grass

This little plant will grow almost anywhere there's a little water and shade. It often creeps into people's potted plants. It's trail nibble for most people, but it is a great substitute for citrus in a pinch.

Flavor Profile

Lemony and citrusy with a light tannic aftertaste. I find the stems to be more tender and juicy than the leaves, and they are a good addition to salads. The flowers are beautiful as a garnish. As the name indicates, they contain oxalic acid, so eating this plant in moderation is key.

When and How to Harvest

Oxalis starts growing during late winter and into early spring in semi-shady fields and under trees. Although you can find oxalis in shady clusters in your garden, they seem to like a woodland ecosystem and can be found most easily in shady forest areas in cooler, more fertile soil. The flowers and leaves are edible as they are, and I utilize the younger plant stems in salads as well.

Oxalis

Distinguishing Identifiers

- Yellow or pink five-petal flowers
- Shamrock-like leaves in threes
- Flower parts in fives
- The leaves close or fold at night or when water is really scarce

Possible Look-Alikes

- Clover (the flowers are entirely different, however)

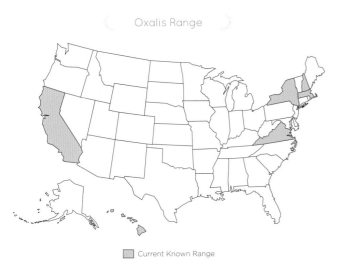

Oxalis Range

Current Known Range

Hillside Herb and Grapefruit Salad

Grapefruit with Wild Chervil and Toasted Coriander

Serves: 2 — Difficulty level: Easy

Although it sounds like an unusual combination, the brightness of the grapefruit, smokiness of the toasted coriander seeds and the delicateness of the chervil and chervil vinegar are a trifecta. This dish is excellent for breakfast or as the topping to a salad or even a savory dessert. I happen to love grapefruit, and this is hands down my favorite way to eat it.

1 tbsp (8 g) whole coriander seeds

2 tbsp (30 ml) Chervil Vinegar (below)

1 tbsp (15 ml) olive oil

2 large grapefruit, sectioned and hollowed-out rinds reserved

1 cup (10 g) chervil, washed and stemmed

Flaked sea salt, to taste

In a small, heavy-bottomed dry pan over medium heat, toast the corriander seeds, moving them constantly, until they just start popping and release their oils, about 2 to 3 minutes. Move the seeds to a cutting board and crack them with the back of a plate or cup (or use a mortar and pestle).

In a small bowl, whisk the chervil vinegar and olive oil together to emulsify. Toss the grapefruit and chervil together with the dressing. Fill the grapefruit halves with the dressed grapefruit and chervil. Top each serving with the cracked coriander seeds and a pinch of flaked salt.

Chervil Vinegar

Makes: 2 cups (480 ml) — Difficulty level: Easy

This vinegar is excellent in a beurre blanc, in dressings and over fish.
Use a light vinegar, such as white wine, champagne or rice vinegar.

2 cups (480 ml) white wine, champagne or rice vinegar

1 cup (10 g) chervil stems and leaves, washed

Pour the vinegar into a medium mason jar or airtight glass container. Bruise the chervil stems lightly with the back of a knife and pack the chervil into the container. Secure the container's lid tightly and give it a good shake. Infuse the vinegar in the refrigerator for 5 to 7 days. Strain the chervil from the vinegar using cheesecloth, not a metal strainer, and discard the chervil. Store chervil vinegar in the refrigerator for up to 6 months.

Field Crunch Salad

Milk Thistle Stems, Fava Beans, Green Almonds and Lemon

Serves: 2 — Difficulty level: Easy

Milk thistle stems are sweet and crunchy, with a flavor reminiscent of artichokes. Harvest the stems using gardening gloves and a sharp knife to cut the base of the stem. You clean the stems much like you would celery: peel back all the strings and fibers to reveal a tender stalk. The stems will darken a bit, just like artichokes, so after you harvest the stems and clean them, store them in acidulated water until just before using or make your dressing first and put the stems and vegetables right into the dressing as you cut them.

1 cup (170 g; 8 to 10 pods) **fresh fava beans**

1 tbsp (14 g) **butter**

1 clove **garlic,** minced

Pinch sea salt

1 tbsp (15 ml) **fresh lemon juice**

1 tbsp (15 ml) **olive oil**

1 medium **shallot, finely minced**

1 tsp **dried oregano**

Pinch sugar or sweetener of your choice

Sea salt and freshly ground black pepper, to taste

1 cup (36 g) **milk thistle stems, cleaned, trimmed and cut into 1-inch (3-cm) pieces**

1 cup (116 g) **daikon ribbons (see note)**

2 cups (86 g) **purslane with stems, washed and roughly chopped**

½ cup (50 g) **green almonds, washed and thinly sliced**

Remove the fava beans from their pods. In a small pot over high heat, blanch the beans in salted, rapidly boiling water for 1 minute and drain. Squeeze or pop the beans from their soft coating shells and set aside.

In a small sauté pan over medium heat, toss the shelled fava beans with the butter, garlic and pinch salt for 1 to 2 minutes, until the beans are coated and a little soft. Set aside.

In a medium bowl, whisk together the lemon juice, olive oil, shallot, oregano, sugar and salt and pepper. Add all the vegetables to the bowl and toss in the dressing, coating everything evenly. Crunch away!

Note: Daikon ribbons are easy to make! Use a vegetable peeler to produce long, thin strips of daikon.

Picked Picnic Salad

Apple, Fennel, Chervil and Potato

Serves: 4 — Difficulty level: Easy

Almost everyone's pantry already has most of the ingredients to make this dish. I'll often make this with a vegan mayo in large batches and bring it to picnics or outdoor events. I have not met anyone who doesn't like it. We have fennel growing everywhere here, along with chervil, and they happen to complement each other nicely. I like recipes that blend sweet and savory, and this one doesn't disappoint. The extra mayo is fantastic as a dip or on garden tomato sandwiches with tons of cracked black pepper.

1 cup (240 ml) olive oil, divided

1 tbsp (15 ml) water

1 tbsp (15 ml) Chervil Vinegar (page 25)

1 large egg yolk

¼ tsp sea salt

1 tsp Prepared Mustard (page 82)

2 cups (20 g) chervil, washed and stemmed, divided

2 medium potatoes, peeled and cut into ½-inch (3-cm) cubes

2 medium green apples, unpeeled, washed, cored and cut into ½-inch (3-cm) cubes

1 small bulb fennel, trimmed and julienned

4 medium apples (any variety), for serving

With an immersion blender and a small bowl or in a small food processor, add ½ cup (120 ml) of the oil, water, chervil vinegar, egg yolk, salt, mustard and 1 cup (10 g) of the chervil and blend for about 1 minute to emulsify. While blending, slowly drizzle in the remaining ½ cup (120 ml) oil. Taste for salt and adjust as needed. Store the mayo in the refrigerator until ready to use.

In a small pot over high heat, cook the potatoes in rapidly boiling salted water for 7 to 10 minutes. Check one of the cubes at 7 minutes to see if it's tender. You want them to be a little firm, but not raw, so they hold up in the salad. Drain the potatoes, let them cool and set aside.

In a medium bowl, combine the potatoes, apples and fennel. Add the mayo and remaining 1 cup (10 g) chervil and fold. Chill for 30 to 60 minutes. Right before serving, cut the top ½ inch (13 mm) off each serving apple. Core and hollow out the apples to make room for your filling. Serve the prepared salad in the apple "cups."

Note: Immediately after cubing the apples and potatoes, toss them in a bowl with a cup (240 ml) of water and a tablespoon (15 ml) of vinegar or lemon juice to keep them from oxidizing.

Spring Harvest Salad

Chickweed, Oxalis, Pistachios and Quail Eggs

Serves: 2-4 — Difficulty level: Easy

This gorgeous salad makes me want to just run a piece of good bread down the plate, collecting anything in its path. The chickweed mimics the peas, the oxalis the lemon; the pistachio-pea puree is light and gives the wispy spring greens some heft; the eggs add richness, the herb dressing brightness; and the buttermilk lends some acidity to this incredible dish.

6 quail eggs

1 cup (123 g) raw pistachios

2 cups (480 ml) cold water

1 cup (151 g) fresh peas, shelled

2 tbsp (30 ml) vegetable stock, divided

¼ tsp plus pinch sea salt, divided, plus more as needed

1 tsp fresh lemon juice

1 clove garlic confit (see sidebar)

2 tbsp (8 g) fresh thyme, tarragon, parsley or basil leaves (or a combination)

2½ tsp (12 ml) olive oil

1 cup (240 ml) buttermilk

2 cups (40 g) oxalis, washed and stemmed

2 cups (80 g) chickweed, washed and trimmed

Fresh thyme, tarragon, parsley or basil leaves (or a combination), for garnish

Freshly ground black pepper, to taste

To prepare the quail eggs, follow the directions for poaching quail eggs on page 107. Soak the raw pistachios in the cold water in the refrigerator for 8 hours or overnight. Drain and remove any pistachio skins by gently rubbing the nuts between kitchen towels. Add the pistachios to a high-speed food processor.

In a small pot over high heat, blanch the peas in vigorously boiling, lightly salted water for 2 to 3 minutes. Strain the peas and add them to the processor along with the pistachios, 1 tablespoon (15 ml) of the vegetable stock, ¼ teaspoon of the salt, lemon juice, garlic, thyme and olive oil. Blend until smooth and satiny. If the mixture isn't thin enough, add the remaining 1 tablespoon (15 ml) vegetable stock, 1 teaspoon at a time. Taste the puree for salt and adjust if needed. Transfer the puree to an airtight container and store it in the refrigerator until ready to use.

To a whipped cream dispenser charged with a nitrous oxide cartridge, add the buttermilk and the remaining pinch salt. Shake vigorously to create a foam and store in the refrigerator. You can also froth the buttermilk and salt in a small bowl using an immersion blender.

To assemble the salad, spread the pistachio-pea puree on a platter or individual plates. Sprinkle the oxalis and chickweed over the top of the puree and gently nestle the quail eggs in the greens. Place the herbs carefully around the plate for garnish. Dot the salad with the buttermilk foam and season with additional salt and pepper to taste.

Garlic Confit

Add 2 to 3 heads of garlic (crush the heads slightly to release the cloves), to a small pot over medium-high heat. Add 1 cup (240 ml) olive oil. The oil should cover the garlic pieces. Bring the oil and garlic to a simmer and then turn the heat down as low as your stove will allow. Cover the saucepan and let this poach for about 1 hour. Turn off the heat and let the oil and garlic cool completely.

"Etc." Sandwich

Eggplant, Tomato and Chickweed

Serves: 2-4 — Difficulty level: Moderate

I really don't like to do anything with chickweed other than eat it as simply as possible. It's just perfect as is in every way. It's tender, sweet, compatible with almost any flavor and so cute. I have noticed that it's also the perfect sandwich green because it stays together in clumps (much like sprouts) and although it's a tender little green, it's pretty hardy. Consider using it to fill wraps and spring rolls, too. I've made eggplant bacon a variety of ways, and here I provide directions for both the stovetop and the oven.

1 tsp brown sugar

1 tsp molasses

Water, as needed

2 tbsp (30 ml) tamari

½ tsp liquid smoke

½ tsp apple cider vinegar

½ tsp Acorn Miso (page 210) or any variety of store-bought miso

Pinch cayenne

Pinch onion powder

Pinch sea salt

2 medium Chinese or Japanese eggplants (any long, skinny variety will work)

4 tbsp (60 ml) grapeseed or other high-heat oil, for frying, divided

Freshly ground black pepper, to taste

Mayo, as needed

Fresh tomato slices, as needed

2 cups (80 g) chickweed, washed

In a small bowl, combine the brown sugar and molasses and enough water to thin out the brown sugar mixture. Once the brown sugar is dissolved, add the tamari, liquid smoke, vinegar, miso, cayenne, onion powder and salt, stirring until the ingredients are dissolved and well combined. Set aside.

Cut the tops and bottoms off the eggplants and discard. With a vegetable slicer or a mandolin, thinly shave or slice around the eggplant, making four sides. You'll probably be able to get about 12 to 14 slices per side. You want to stop slicing each side when you start to reach seeds. You can save the eggplant centers to make a dip later or add them to soups or stews.

If you are making the eggplant bacon on the stovetop, heat 2 tablespoons (30 ml) of the oil in a large sauté pan over medium-high heat. When the oil is hot, but not smoking, brush one side of each of the eggplant strips with the brown sugar mixture and carefully lay the strips down in the oil, seasoned-side up, and cook for 2 minutes or until a bit crisp. Flip the pieces and fry the other side for 1 minute. Drain the cooked eggplant bacon on kitchen paper. You may need to wipe the pan for burnt bits before frying the next batch with the remaining 2 tablespoons (30 ml) oil.

To serve, slather your toast or roll with the mayo of your choice. Add the eggplant bacon and tomato slices to the sandwich and top the tomatoes very generously with the chickweed.

Succulents and Scallops

Purslane, Scallops and Tomato Butter Dressing

Serves: 2 — Difficulty level: Easy

I love the succulent pop and crunch of purslane and sea beans. You can forage sea beans (*Salicornia*) in certain parts of the country and find them at better farmers' markets and specialty markets. It's not unheard of for people to grow them in their gardens. Sea beans are not necessary to this particular recipe, as purslane gives the same juicy, almost salty pop, but I include them in case you have access to them. Sea beans are not something I typically harvest, but I always look for them at the market.

2 tbsp (30 ml) white wine vinegar

2 tsp (10 ml) honey

1 cup (240 g) canned whole tomatoes with juice, pureed

¾ tsp plus pinch sea salt, divided

8–10 large bay or sea scallops, shucked and cleaned, divided

2 tbsp (28 g) plus 2 tsp (10 g) butter, divided

2 tsp (10 ml) olive oil, divided

1 clove garlic, minced

1 tbsp (5 g) finely chopped fresh basil

2 cups (86 g) purslane, washed and trimmed into 1-inch (3-cm) sections

1 cup (150 g) sea beans, cleaned and soaked

In a small saucepan over medium heat, add the vinegar and reduce it by half, about 7 to 10 minutes. Add the honey and bring the mixture to a simmer. Add the tomato puree, stir vigorously, and reduce by half again, another 7 to 10 minutes. Add ½ teaspoon of the salt and carefully taste for seasoning. The mixture should be sweet, salty, tart and syrupy and taste like concentrated tomatoes. Take the saucepan off the heat and set aside.

Pat the scallops dry and salt them on both sides with ¼ teaspoon of the salt. Add 1 teaspoon of the butter and 1 teaspoon of the oil to a large sauté pan over medium-high heat. When the pan is very hot, almost smoking, add half of the scallops and sear on each side for 1 to 2 minutes. Don't move the scallops around; let them crust and release before turning them to sear on the other side for 1 minute. Set the scallops aside on kitchen paper. Repeat this process with the remaining 1 teaspoon butter and 1 teaspoon oil. Turn off the heat and add the remaining 2 tablespoons (28 g) butter, the garlic, basil and the remaining pinch salt and melt, swirling the pan to flavor the butter for 1 minute.

Assemble the salad by placing 4 to 5 scallops on each plate and arranging the purslane and sea beans around the scallops. Drizzle the garlic-basil butter over the scallops and the tomato sauce over the entire salad. Add more fresh herbs and freshly cracked black pepper if you'd like. The warm scallops and cold, succulent vegetables are a nice contrast.

Note: I usually plunge my purslane and sea beans in ice water right before serving for an extra crunch. Drain them well and shake off excess water.

Fish and *field* Pie

Potato, Sole and Chervil

Serves: 6–8 — Difficulty level: Moderate

This is a simple dish, but there's a bit of prep involved. It does make the entire house smell so comforting and welcoming, though, so the prep work is worth it. This recipe is basically a one-pot wonder and is certainly hearty enough for dinner. The recipe calls for a lot of chervil, but it really works. It is a very subtle herb, and it permeates the cream beautifully and is a nice combination with the slightly anisey vermouth.

2 large russet potatoes, peeled

4 tbsp (56 g) butter, cold, divided

1 tbsp (8 g) all-purpose flour

3 medium shallots, peeled and minced

2 cloves garlic, minced

¼ cup (60 ml) dry vermouth

1½ cups (360 ml) heavy cream

½ tsp sea salt

2 (4-oz [112-g]) fillets of sole

3 cups (30 g) chervil, washed and stemmed, plus more for garnish

Preheat the oven to 350°F (177°C).

Prepare a 7-inch (18-cm) spring form pan by cutting a round piece of parchment paper for the bottom and greasing the sides and bottom well.

Using a mandolin, carefully slice the potatoes crosswise on the thinnest possible setting or the potatoes will not cook through. Place the potato slices in a bowl of cold water while slicing the others, as they will oxidize.

Make a beurre manié by combining and kneading together 1 tablespoon (14 g) of the butter and the flour. Form 2 balls and set aside.

In a small sauté pan, sauté the shallots in 1 tablespoon (14 g) of the butter on medium-low heat until translucent, about 4 to 5 minutes. Add the garlic and cook another minute. Add the vermouth and reduce the mixture by one third (about 7 to 10 minutes). Add the cream and salt and bring to a light simmer, but do not boil. Whisk in one of the balls of the beurre manié. Stir for 2 to 3 minutes—the mixture should thicken slightly. You want the sauce to be the consistency of light pancake batter. If it does not tighten up enough, whisk in the other ball of the beurre manié and cook for another 3 to 4 minutes. Taste for salt and adjust as needed.

Slice the sole into very thin bite-size pieces. Assemble the pie by forming a thin and even layer of the potato slices in a circular pattern, 2 tablespoons (30 ml) of the cream mixture, another layer of potato slices, a pinch salt, a few of the fish pieces, 2 tablespoons (30 ml) of the cream mixture and one-fourth of the chervil. Repeat this process and reserve enough potato slices to cover the top. Pour the remaining liquid over the top and gently poke a few holes sporadically with a bamboo skewer on top so the liquid soaks to the bottom. Bake the pie, covered, for 1 hour. Uncover and dot the pie with the remaining 2 tablespoons (28 g) butter and cook for another 15 to 20 minutes to brown on top. Let the pie cool all the way before removing it from the spring form pan. Garnish the pie with additional chervil. This dish is wonderful reheated, but it's also lovely at room temperature with a squeeze of lemon.

forest Fritto Misto

Mustard, Curly Dock, Nettles and Lambsquarters

Serves: 2 — Difficulty level: Easy

Sometimes the simplest applications are the best. I like this dish when entertaining people who are new to eating harvested or foraged foods—it's approachable and it's fried, for goodness' sake. This is another dish you can make with things you have on hand. I make this with a quick blender aioli using preserves that I've made with harvests from other times in the year, such as wild currant jam or pickled green walnuts. When frying like this, using larger, slightly older leaves is fine as they can stand up to this cooking technique. I use the leaves I have available to me, but this can be adapted to pretty much any edible leaf, including grape leaves, which are especially nice when fried this way. You could also fry a few elderflower umbels this way and include them in the mix.

8 cups (1.9 L) grapeseed oil or other high-heat oil, for frying

3 cups (300 g) plus 4 tbsp (30 g) sifted cake flour or superfine flour, divided

4–6 large mustard or radish leaves, washed, with stems

2–4 small curly dock leaves, washed, with stems

4–6 large nettle leaves, washed

4–6 large lambsquarters leaves, washed

2 large eggs

2 cups (480 ml) ice water

Sea salt, to taste

Wild Currant Aioli (page 36), to serve

I always use a mini deep fryer for this as it's cleaner, I can control the temperature and remove the leaves more efficiently. However, if you don't own a mini deep fryer, you can use a large cast iron pan and fill it with about 2 inches (6 cm) of high-heat oil.

Fill the mini deep fryer to the maximum oil level indicated by the machine and preheat it to 360°F (182°C). Add 4 tablespoons (30 g) of the flour to a plate and set it within reach of the mini deep fryer (you will dredge the leaves in the flour prior to frying them).

Wash the mustard leaves, curly dock leaves, nettle leaves and lambsquarters leaves and pat them dry, leaving a little moisture on them.

Crack the eggs into a large bowl and break them gently with a fork. Add the water, ice and all, and gently combine the eggs and water. Sprinkle the remaining 3 cups (300 g) flour over the surface of the mixture and stir as little as possible. I use a silicon spatula to tap it into the water. The goal is to stir this as little as possible while combining to form a batter. The consistency should coat a spoon but still be a reasonably thin batter and there will be a few clumps of flour that remain. That's OK.

Press both sides of the mustard leaves, curly dock leaves, nettle leaves and lambsquarters leaves into the flour on the plate. A little flour should stick to the remaining moisture on the leaves. Quickly dunk them into the batter, shaking off any excess (this is important) and lower them gently into the fryer. Fry until the leaves are lightly browned, about 1½ or 2 minutes. Depending on your fryer, you can probably fry 3 leaves at a time. Drain the fried leaves on kitchen paper and salt them immediately.

Serve the leaves right away on a plate with crunchy salts and a beautiful, rich aioli and some ice-cold beer. This is a nice conversation starter as you can explain to your guests what they are eating.

Wild Currant Aioli

Rustic, Rich Mayo with Tart Wild Currants

Makes: about 1 cup (220 g) — **Difficulty level:** Easy

An aioli, in my opinion, is a slightly thicker, more rustic mayo, but for all intents and purposes, it's the same thing. The first time I ever attempted an aioli, I used Alice Waters' recipe in a mortar and pestle. You can do that and it's wonderful—but it's quicker to make with a small hand blender. Also, you can use anything you'd like to flavor the aioli or just enjoy its simple garlicky goodness. I have adapted this recipe by decreasing the garlic a bit and adding some tangy dried currants that I harvested and reconstituted in wine. With some (preferably homemade) currant jam folded in, this aioli gets even better.

⅛ cup (19 g) dried currants

¼ cup (60 ml) dry white wine

1 clove garlic

¼ tsp Himalayan salt flakes or Maldon salt

1 large egg yolk

¾ cup (180 ml) olive oil

1 tsp currant jam, optional

In a small bowl, soak the dried currants in the wine for at least 2 hours or up to overnight. Drain the currants and roughly chop them. Reserve the wine.

On a cutting board, smash the garlic with the heel of a heavy knife blade or a pestle. Once the garlic is smashed, add the salt and grind the salt into the garlic, breaking it up and making a rough paste. Scrape the garlic-salt mixture into a small bowl and whisk in the egg yolk and ½ teaspoon of the reserved wine. Combine well. Transfer this mixture to a small food processor or an immersion blender with a cup attachment and blend while slowly adding a few drops of oil at a time until the mixture thickens. Very slowly drizzle in the rest of the olive oil. If the aioli is too thick, add a few drops of the reserved wine. Taste for salt and adjust if necessary.

Fold in the chopped currants and currant jam and serve with the Forest Fritto Misto (page 34). This is also fantastic with leftover chicken in a chicken salad sandwich.

Cheese and Crackers Pie with *Oxalis*

Preserved Lemon and Chèvre Cheesecake and Oxalis

Serves: 4-6 — Difficulty Level: Easy

I wanted to create a casual dish to eat while I sat around with friends and had some wine. I had some wonderful goat chèvre and crème fraîche made by a friend, some crackers and a lush little patch of lemony oxalis. The oxalis is more than a beautiful garnish—it's a much-needed lemony green to foil the creamy richness of the cheese. This is a great alternative to cheese and crackers and a substantial little cocktail snack you can make as minis or as a small cheesecake.

2 large eggs, divided

4 tbsp (56 g) butter

1 cup (59 g) saltine cracker crumbs

2 cups (425 g) chèvre

2 tbsp (15 g) crème fraîche

2 tbsp (18 g) cornstarch

1 tbsp (15 ml) honey

1½ tbsp (2 g) finely chopped preserved lemon

¼ tsp sea salt, optional

1½ cups (30 g) oxalis leaves, washed and stemmed

Preheat the oven to 300°F (175°C).

Crack one of the eggs into a small measuring cup. Crack open the other egg and separate the yolk from the white, adding the yolk to the whole egg in the measuring cup. Beat the whole egg and egg yolk to combine. Add the separated egg white to a small bowl and beat it lightly. Set aside.

Melt the butter in a small pot over medium heat and let it cool. Combine the melted butter with the beaten egg white and the cracker crumbs.

Prepare a 5-inch (13-cm) spring form pan by lining the bottom with circle of parchment paper. Press the cracker crumb mixture into the bottom of the locked spring form pan and bake on a baking sheet for 8 to 10 minutes. Remove the crust from the oven and let it cool in the pan.

While the crust is pre-baking, combine the chèvre, crème fraîche, cornstarch, honey and preserved lemon in a food processor and pulse until smooth. Taste for salt. The preserved lemon can be salty enough. Adjust the seasoning with the optional salt if necessary. Add the beaten egg yolk mixture and pulse until smooth (about 2 to 3 minutes).

Lower the oven temperature to 250°F (121°C).

Grease the sides of the spring form pan, pour the chèvre batter on top of the baked crust and gently lift the pan and drop it on the counter to release any air bubbles. Bake for 1 hour. The cake will jiggle slightly in the center, but it should be firm. Cover the top of the pie with the oxalis. Slice and serve with some red onion, smoked fish and lots of wine.

Nasturtium Hiyayakko Salad

Nasturtium, Tofu and Bonito

Serves: 4 — Difficulty level: Easy

I don't eat much tofu and it's not a staple for me; however, the first time I had this dish at a Japanese café many years ago, I decided that this would be my tofu dish. I have interpreted it here by making a green, creamy and spicy sauce with the silky tofu and fresh nasturtium topped with wispy shaved bonito and toppings.

The tofu and its creaminess are an integral part of the dish and all the components you put on it are equally important. That said, all the ingredients have to be of pristine quality as there are so few of them. Start with some good-quality, organic silken tofu. I serve this as a starter or with some soup for lunch.

1 (14-oz [397-g]) package silken tofu, divided

2 tbsp (30 ml) water

2 cups (40 g) densely packed nasturtium leaves, washed, plus 6 leaves and or flowers for garnish

1 tsp tamari

1 tbsp (15 ml) fresh lemon juice

Pinch sea salt

¼ tsp olive oil

¼ tsp brown rice syrup or agave

½ medium shallot, minced

1 cup (150 g) cherry tomatoes, washed and halved

2 tsp (10 ml) ponzu sauce (see note)

4 tbsp (4 g) bonito flakes

4 tsp (4 g) furikake, optional (see note)

Pickled ginger, optional

Sesame seeds, optional

Scallions, optional

In a small food processor or personal blender, add 2 ounces (57 g) of the tofu, the water, nasturtium, tamari, lemon juice, salt, oil, brown rice syrup and shallot. Blend until smooth and frothy. It should be the consistency of a thin salad dressing. If it's not thin enough, add more water, 1 teaspoon at a time. Taste for seasoning and adjust as needed.

Divide the remaining 12 ounces (342 g) chilled tofu into even portions in rectangles on plates and spoon the sauce over the tofu. Top the tofu with the tomatoes, ponzu, nasturtium leaves, bonito flakes and furikake. You can add pickled ginger, sesame seeds and scallions or any other fresh vegetables you'd like.

Note: Ponzu sauce is a Japanese citrus-based, soy-like sauce. Furikake is a Japanese blend of ground fish, seaweed, sesame seeds and spices.

Wild "Wasabi" Salad

Nasturtium, Salmon Crudo Salad and Apples

Serves: 4 — Difficulty level: Easy

I love the silky mildness of fresh, raw, sushi-grade salmon. Its rich fattiness combined with the peppery bite of the nasturtium, fresh green apples, crispy salmon skin and a little bit of homemade honey mustard dressing is delicious. This dish requires no cooking, just really fresh, high-quality fish and just-harvested nasturtiums.

1 (8-oz [227-g]) fillet of sushi-grade salmon with skin, descaled

1 tbsp (15 ml) plus 1 tsp grapeseed or other high-heat oil

1 tsp fresh lemon juice

Water, as needed

2 medium Granny Smith apples or other tart, firm green apples, unpeeled, washed and cored

½ tbsp (8 ml) honey

2 tbsp (30 ml) apple cider vinegar

½ tsp plus pinch sea salt

1 tsp Prepared Mustard (page 82)

½ medium shallot, minced

8 cups (160 g) nasturtium leaves, washed and stemmed

Freshly ground black pepper, to taste

Ask your fishmonger to remove and reserve the salmon skin or carefully remove it yourself with a sharp fillet knife. Cut the salmon skin crosswise into thin strips with a very sharp knife. In a medium sauté pan, heat the oil over medium-high heat. After about 3 to 4 minutes, test a piece of the salmon skin and see if it sizzles in the oil. The oil's temperature should be about 365°F (185°C). When the oil is hot enough, fry the pieces of salmon skin until browned, 2 to 3 minutes. The skin will sizzle and pop depending on the fat content. Drain the skin on kitchen paper and salt lightly. Set aside until you are ready to serve.

Cut the fillet of salmon into 1 x 1½–inch (3 x 4-cm) strips against the grain and store them in the refrigerator, covered, until you are ready to serve.

Prepare a small bowl by adding the lemon juice and 3 to 4 tablespoons (45 to 60 ml) of water and stir to combine. Cut the tops and bottoms off the apples and discard. Core the apple, and using a mandolin on the finest possible setting, shave thin, circular slices of the apples and set them in the bowl of lemon water to keep them from browning.

In another small bowl, whisk together the honey, vinegar, salt, and mustard until smooth and combined. It will emulsify a bit with vigorous whisking. Fold in the shallot.

Assemble your salad by arranging a bed of nasturtium and apples, topped by the raw salmon. Generously spoon the dressing over the top of the salad and top it with cracked pepper to taste, the salmon skins and any nasturtium or wild flowers, if you have them.

Watercress Granita

Watercress, Lemon and Ice

Serves: 2-4 — Difficulty level: Easy

This dish is an extremely refreshing palate cleanser or light dessert. The tart pepperiness of the granita with sweet summer strawberries is unusual and memorable and so easy to prepare.

¾ cup (144 g) sugar

½ cup (120 ml) fresh lemon juice

1 tbsp (15 ml) rice wine vinegar

2-4 tbsp (30-60 ml) water, or as needed

2 cups (68 g) watercress leaves and stems, washed and roughly chopped

Pinch sea salt

In a small pot over low heat, dissolve the sugar with the lemon juice, about 2 to 3 minutes and let cool. Once the lemon mixture has cooled, combine it with the vinegar, 2 tablespoons (30 ml) of the water, watercress and salt in a high-speed blender or processor and liquefy the ingredients. It should be the consistency of a smoothie. Add additional water, 1 tablespoon (15 ml) at a time, if the mixture is not thin enough. Let this mixture sit in the refrigerator for at least 20 to 30 minutes so the watercress can release its flavors.

Strain the mixture through a medium-grain sieve (it's fine to have little watercress pieces). Pour the granita mixture into a 4-cup (960-ml) glass dish suitable for freezing and cover the dish with plastic wrap. After 2 hours, start scraping the granita with a fork and continue to do so every 30 minutes until you have a dish of snow-like granita. Fluff the granita right before serving.

Chapter Three

Unexpected flavor Doppelgangers

Plantain, Mallow and Cattail

Reading about nature is fine, but if a person walks in the woods and listens carefully, he can learn more than what is in books.

– George Washington Carver

The reason I grouped these plants together is that they resemble other plants in flavor, but not in appearance. To me, young plantain, when cooked, tastes and has a similar texture to wakame (seaweed); mallow has a similar flavor and texture to okra; and cattail shoots have a similar flavor to cucumbers, while the cattail flowers have a flavor not unlike corn. Remarkably, they are great substitutes to these more common vegetables. I also grouped them together because I find that they can be the most unapproachable in terms of what the heck to do with them.

Perhaps with the exception of cattail, plantain and mallow aren't among the "forager's first picks." But they are so abundantly available, especially mallow, that I really wanted to find a few special dishes for them to highlight how versatile they can be other than as a potherb.

Plantain

Plantago major

Plantaginaceae family
(formerly Figwort family)

Native to Europe and northern and southern Asia; introduced, naturalized and invasive; grows worldwide

Not related to the banana-type fruit (cooking plantains)

Plantain field (*Plantago major*)

anywhere and in a variety of climates, but I tend to find them most commonly in compact, clay-heavy soils (e.g., dried river, stream or lake beds) in dappled or shady conditions. Your best bet is to find them growing near a current or former water source.

Flavor Profile

The young shoots and leaves are tender. As they get older, the fibrous veins get too tough to break down with cooking. In its raw state, plantain really doesn't have much flavor, but blanched for 3 minutes in lightly salted water, it becomes slightly translucent and has a faint flavor and smell of seaweed, as well as a similar texture. That's the texture you want.

When and How to Harvest

Harvest the young leaves near the base or the single new shoots with a sharp pair of scissors or pruners. They can grow in almost any environment—you can find them almost

Distinguishing Identifiers

- Distinctive parallel vein patterns on the leaves (almost striped)

- Ovate, broad basal leaves

- Low-to-the-ground green plant with inconspicuous flowers

Possible Look-Alikes

- Woolly plantain (*Plantago patagonica*)

- Common evening primrose (*Oenothera biennis*)

Common Mallow

Malva neglecta

Malvaceae family

Introduced and invasive;
grows worldwide

Also called cheeseweed, cheeseplant
and buttonweed

Related to marshmallow
and okra

Common mallow field (*Malva neglecta*)

Flavor Profile

I like the flavor of raw mallow, although the leaves can be a little tough. Selecting the younger leaves is optimal, but I do use the older ones if I am stewing them down for long periods of time or frying. The flavor of mallow leaves very much resembles the taste of okra leaves. It cooks down quickly and can act as a slight thickener depending on the preparation. Before they flower, the young buds are delicious raw and taste a little like raw asparagus. They deepen in flavor slightly when cooked. The seeds are also edible after roasting.

Common Mallow Range

Current Known Range

When and How to Harvest

Mallow makes an appearance in late spring and early summer, but I see it lingering in people's yards almost until fall if it's not too hot and year-round if it has a water source. It's a very hardy plant and loves direct sunlight, but it will die out in extreme heat. You can find mallow covering entire fields in harsh, dry soils. Not a foraged plant that hides, common mallow is often found in plain sight on roadsides and the sides of trails.

Mallow is one of those plants that starts wilting the minute you harvest it. It will come back by soaking the stems for 10 minutes in cold water.

Distinguishing Identifiers

- Alternate leaves that are rounded and lobe-edged
- Red dot in the center of the leaf, attached to the stem
- Funnel-shaped flowers
- Mucilaginous or slightly slimy quality when crushed

Possible Look-Alikes

- Hollyhocks (also in the Malvaceae family)
- Varieties of geraniums and hibiscus

Cattail

Typha

Typhaceae family

Native to Canada and both native and
introduced in the United States

Native to Canada and both native and introduced in the
United States; there are several main species: broad leaf,
narrow and common, and there are hybrids between them, as
well; certain species are very aggressively invasive depending
on your region; *Typha* is found worldwide

Flavor Profile

So many parts of this plant are edible, including the flowers
(or cobs), pollen, shoots and roots. The flowers have a boiled
corn-like flavor, the shoots have the flavor of cucumber and
aloe, the pollen is flavorless for the most part except for a very
slight grassy note and the roots are mainly used for starch.

Cattail patch (*Typha*)

When and How to Harvest

This is a plant that is riparian—it likes river and stream beds, as
well as marshes. I mainly use the shoots and pollen, but there
are uses for the roots, as well. I look for small to medium tender
shoots near the middle of a cattail cluster. It's a little bit of work,
but find your way to the bottom of the shoot and give it a firm
pull straight up. Unless you dig out the root, the shoot should
break off just above the root. Make a clean cut to that end and
trim off the green, leafy, inedible top part of the stalk. Like a
leek, you peel away the outer fibrous layers until you reach the
tender core. Soak the trimmed cattail stalks in several changes
of clean water for 20 minutes each time.

Distinguishing Identifiers

- Reed-like shape and flat, long leaves

- Distinctive yellow-green flowers

- Grows in rivers and marshes

Possible Look-Alikes

- Giant reed (*Arundo donax*)

- **Irises** (highly toxic)

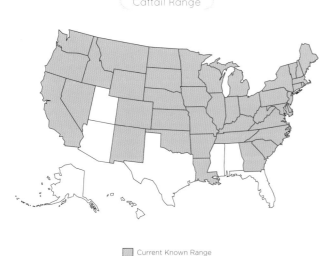

Cattail Range

☐ Current Known Range

Mallow Pop 'n' Crunch

Amaranth Seed–Crusted Mallow Leaves

Serves: 2-4 — Difficulty Level: Easy

This starter, appetizer or snack is a great use for older, larger and tougher mallow leaves, as it can withstand deep frying. Also, you can use a variety of wild seeds, such as amaranth, nettle, plantain or lambsquarters—even quinoa. Here, I use store-bought amaranth seeds. The "chips" have a vegetable flavor that combines nicely with the nuttiness of the popped seeds.

Vegetable oil, for frying

2 tbsp (18 g) cornstarch

3 tbsp (30 g) white rice flour

Pinch sea salt

Pinch sugar

2 tbsp (30 ml) ice-cold water, divided

½ cup (97 g) amaranth seeds

2 cups (30 g) washed and dried mallow leaves

In a small heavy-bottomed pot or a mini deep fryer, preheat the oil to 355°F (179°C). (If using a pot, use approximately 2 cups [480 ml] oil; if using a mini deep fryer, fill it with the minimum amount of oil recommended by the manufacturer.)

In a medium bowl, combine the cornstarch, rice flour, salt, sugar and 1 tablespoon (15 ml) of the cold water and whisk until the mixture is smooth with no lumps. It should have the consistency of a thin pancake batter. Add the remaining 1 tablespoon (15 ml) water if it's too thick. Spread the amaranth seeds on a small, flat plate. Dip the leaves quickly into the batter and shake off any excess batter. The leaves should have a very thin layer. Coat one side of each leaf with the amaranth seeds by pressing them into the plate. Add 2 to 3 leaves at a time to the hot oil. (If your oil is not hot enough, the amaranth seeds will fall off and the leaves will wilt and become greasy.) The amaranth seeds will toast and pop in the oil and may splatter a bit. Drain the fried leaves on paper towels and lightly salt them when they are still hot.

Serve immediately either on their own or with some Wild Currant Aioli (page 36).

Moroccan Mallow Bastilla

Mallow and Quail with Saffron, Fried Almonds, Eggs and Cinnamon

Serves: 2-4 — Difficulty level: Advanced

Moroccan food is so special and mysterious to me. Having traveled there as a child, I felt it was so different to anywhere I'd ever been, and the shapes, colors, smells and sounds were so magical and vivid to me. Bastilla was the first dish I had that crossed every line and boundary between sweet and savory. My mind was blown and this single dish made an impression on me that still resonates today. In addition, mallow is also a weed that grows in that region of the world and they make some wonderful dishes with it.

The ingredients for this dish are simple, but there are quite a few steps if you are making this from scratch. This is definitely a special-occasion dish. If I could summarize the flavor profile of the dish, it would be minced chicken over a fragrant omelet laden with saffron, orange-blossom water, turmeric, ginger and fried almonds, all wrapped in phyllo dough dusted with cinnamon and sugar. It sounds like a complicated combination, but it works. I use semi-boneless quail halves. They have just the tiny leg bone and the rest of the meat is tied in a "knot" like a lollipop, keeping it juicy and moist during cooking. You can serve this dish to four people as an appetizer or two people as an entrée.

Note: You can, of course, make this easy and add some chicken, cut into pieces, and bake the dish in a standard pie tin or spring form pan.

1 (8-oz [227-g]) roll frozen phyllo sheets

1½ tsp (8 g) plus pinch sea salt, divided

4 cups (60 g) mallow leaves, washed and stemmed

2 large eggs, beaten

¼ tsp orange-blossom water

4 tbsp (60 ml) vegetable oil, divided

½ cup (54 g) blanched slivered almonds

2 medium quails, semi-boneless, cut in half to make 4 pieces

1 small sweet onion, peeled and thinly sliced

1 tsp ground cinnamon, plus more for garnish

½ tsp finely grated fresh ginger

½ tsp fresh turmeric, grated finely with a micro plane

6 tbsp (84 g) butter, divided

1 tsp saffron stigmas

1 tbsp (8 g) powdered sugar

Thaw out the phyllo sheets per the package's instructions.

In a small pot over high heat, combine ½ teaspoon of the salt with 8 cups (1.9 L) water and bring the water to a boil. Blanch the mallow in the water for 2 to 3 minutes. Drain the mallow but reserve 2 tablespoons (30 ml) of the cooking water and, when the leaves are cool enough to handle, roughly chop them and set aside.

In a small bowl, add the eggs, the orange-blossom water and the pinch salt and beat until well combined. Set aside.

Heat 3 tablespoons (45 ml) of the oil in a small heavy-bottomed saucepan or cast iron pan and carefully fry the almonds until they are browned (about 1 to 2 minutes), being careful not to burn them. Remove the almonds from the pan with a slotted spoon the second they start browning and drain them on paper towels. Leave the excess oil in the pan to sear the quails.

(continued)

Lightly salt the quails with ½ teaspoon of the salt and quickly sear them in the pan on all sides until they are slightly brown, 1 to 2 minutes maximum. Remove the quails from the heat and set aside.

Turn the temperature down to medium heat, letting the pan and oil cool down for a few minutes, and sauté the onion with the remaining ½ teaspoon salt, cinnamon, ginger and turmeric until the onion is translucent, about 5 to 7 minutes. You should have enough oil left in the pan, but use the remaining 1 tablespoon (15 ml) oil if needed. Add the mallow and the reserved cooking water and cook for another 2 to 3 minutes or until most of the liquid has evaporated. Remove the vegetables and set aside. Let the pan cool and wipe it out thoroughly.

Heat the pan over low heat and melt 2 tablespoons (28 g) of the butter. Add the saffron. Stir and let the heat pull out the color from the saffron for 4 to 5 minutes. Swirl the butter around the pan evenly and pour in the egg mixture and let it cook for 2 to 3 minutes, folding the mixture occasionally. You want to end up with a soft, loose omelet. Set the omelet aside until you are ready to assemble the dish.

Preheat the oven to 375°F (191°C).

In a small pot over low heat, melt the remaining 4 tablespoons (56 g) butter and have a pastry brush handy.

Brush the wells of a cupcake tin with the melted butter. I use spring form muffin tins, but if you don't have them, you can use parchment cupcake liners. They will make it easier to remove the individual bastillas from the pan.

Roll out the phyllo dough sheets on a cutting board. Cut the sheets into 4 equal squares or as close to that as you can get. Cover the dough with a damp kitchen towel to prevent the cut sheets from drying out while you work.

Brush each piece of phyllo with melted butter and lay 6 pieces (buttered-side down) in the bottom of each cupcake tin as the base. Spoon in one-fourth of the vegetable mixture, 1 teaspoon of the fried almonds, one-fourth of the saffron egg mixture and nestle the quail leg inside each bastilla. Brush 6 more pieces of phyllo with melted butter and drape them over the top of the quail to cover the bastillas. Bake for 20 to 25 minutes or until browned on top.

Garnish the cooked bastillas with additional cinnamon, the powdered sugar and the rest of the fried almonds. Serve with spicy olives and some ice-cold mint tea.

*See photo on page 44.

f'Okra (Faux Okra) Stuffed Crab

Mallow, Corn, Tomato and Crab

Serves: 2-4 — Difficulty Level: Moderate

I love the flavors of summer and this dish pretty much encapsulates them all. It reminds me a little of a deconstructed gumbo meeting a giant crab cake. The mallow in this recipe stands in beautifully for okra and has the same flavor profile, as it's in the same family. This recipe can be easy if you let your fishmonger steam and remove all the meat for you, but I'll say it's moderate or difficult if you do that yourself (especially if you've never done it before). I have a very good fishmonger who does this for me and I can put this dish together in no time. This makes an excellent appetizer or first course. I use a Dungeness crab.

1 (2-lb [910-g]) crab or ½ lb (228 g) crab meat, crab shell reserved

2 tbsp (30 ml) olive oil

1 small onion, cut into ¼-inch (6-mm) pieces

1 small celery stalk, cut into ¼-inch (6-mm) pieces

1 medium green or red bell pepper, cut into ½-inch (13-mm) pieces

1 tsp plus pinch sea salt, divided

1 clove garlic, minced

1 tsp fresh thyme, finely chopped

1 tbsp (5 g) fresh parsley, roughly chopped

4 cups (60 g) mallow, washed, stemmed and roughly chopped, plus more for garnish

2 cups (289 g) fresh corn kernels

½ cup (120 g) Italian diced tomatoes

¼ cup (60 ml) milk

4 tbsp (56 g) butter, divided

4 tbsp (32 g) all-purpose flour

½ tsp cayenne

1 tsp sweet paprika

Pinch white pepper

¾ cup (81 g) panko breadcrumbs

1 tsp roughly chopped fresh cilantro

Clean the crab shell out for presentation and set the crab meat aside, taking care to remove any small bits of loose shell.

Heat the oil in a medium sauté pan over medium heat. Add the onion, celery, bell pepper and ½ teaspoon of the salt. Cook until the vegetables are soft, about 5 minutes. Add the garlic, thyme and parsley and cook 1 more minute. Add the mallow, corn and tomatoes and cook until most of the moisture in the bottom of the pan is gone, about 6 to 7 minutes. Taste for salt, adjusting as needed, transfer the mixture to a medium mixing bowl and set aside.

To make a béchamel sauce, heat the milk in a small pot over medium-high heat until it's just scalded. Take it off the heat and set aside. Using the same pan you used to cook down the vegetables, over medium heat, melt 2 tablespoons (28 g) of the butter and whisk in the flour until melted and combined but not browned, about 2 to 3 minutes. Whisk in the hot milk, ½ teaspoon of the salt, cayenne, paprika and white pepper and bring the mixture to a boil. Reduce the heat to medium and cook 2 to 3 minutes, whisking until the sauce thickens. Taste for salt and adjust accordingly. Turn off the heat, cover the sauce and set aside.

In a small pot over medium heat, melt 1 tablespoon (14 g) of the butter, add the remaining pinch of salt and then toss the breadcrumbs to coat thoroughly. Set aside.

Preheat the oven to 400°F (204°C).

(continued)

f'Okra (Faux Okra) Stuffed Crab (Cont.)

In a large bowl, combine the béchamel sauce and the corn mixture. Gently fold in the crab. Place the crab shell on a medium baking sheet lined with parchment paper, stuff the shell with the corn-crab mixture, spoon the breadcrumbs over the top and dot the breadcrumbs with the remaining 1 tablespoon (14 g) butter. If there's any of the corn-crab mixture left, you can add it to a small ramekin and top with more breadcrumbs and butter and cook it along with the crab shell.

Bake the stuffed crab for 20 to 25 minutes or until lightly browned on top. Garnish with the cilantro and serve family-style with some lemon wedges and steamed asparagus or a light salad.

Mallow Bud Mandilli di Seta

Mallow Buds, Fresh Pasta Sheets and Buttermilk Sauce

Serves: 4–6 — Difficulty level: Advanced

This is an excellent breakfast dish. It's pretty light and healthy and uses one of my favorite forages, mallow buds (the tender immature flower buds). Their flavor is similar to asparagus, artichoke and okra, and they possess a nice, firm but tender texture. The sauce is reminiscent of good old-fashioned ranch dressing with the slight acidity of buttermilk and herbs. I added fresh turmeric for color, but you can omit it.

PASTA

1 cup (175 g) semolina flour, plus more for rolling out pasta

½ cup (65 g) whole wheat sprouted flour

½ cup (63 g) all-purpose flour, plus more for rolling out pasta

¼ tsp sea salt

3 egg yolks, beaten

1–2 tbsp (15–30 ml) water, plus more as needed

2 tbsp (30 ml) olive oil

Note: You do need to pick the mallow buds at the right time, before they start to form a flower and become tough and fibrous.

PASTA

In a food processor with a dough blade or a stand mixer with a dough hook, add the semolina flour, whole wheat flour, all-purpose flour and salt and pulse a few times to sift and aerate. Slowly drizzle in the egg yolks until well incorporated. Add the water, 1 teaspoon at a time, until the dough just comes together into a tight ball in the machine. (You may not need all the water.) Knead the dough in the machine for 6 to 7 minutes until smooth and elastic.

Remove the dough from the machine, form it into two discs, wrap each one tightly in plastic wrap and refrigerate them overnight so that the flours have time to absorb all the liquid and hydrate.

When ready to make, remove one of the dough discs from the refrigerator and, on a lightly floured work surface, roll the pasta out into a large triangle and cut it into 3 to 4 strips. Run each of the strips through the pasta machine (dust the pasta machine rollers with flour as well), once on the biggest setting, once on the second biggest and so on until you have run it through the smallest. (My machine has four settings.) You should end up with long, thin strips. Cut them into square pieces resembling small handkerchiefs. Dust the work surface with a little more semolina flour and lay the "handkerchiefs" on the board so they don't stick.

When cooking this king of pasta, I find that using a large, deep sauté-type pan is better and easier than using a deep pot. Bring some moderately salted water and the oil to a gentle boil. Working with 2 sheets at a time, cook the fresh pasta for 3 to 4 minutes, making sure the pasta sheets do not touch. Gently remove the sheets with a long fish spatula or large spider strainer to drain and place them on a lightly oiled tray, platter or large plate.

Note: You can roll out the dough with a rolling pin, but for this pasta shape, you want to try to get the dough as thin as possible and a pasta machine works really well for this.

BUTTERMILK SAUCE

1 cup (100 g) young mallow buds, washed and trimmed

3 cups (720 ml) buttermilk

½ tsp apple cider vinegar

1 tsp grated fresh turmeric, optional

¼ tsp dried dill

1 tsp dried chives

⅛ tsp onion powder

⅛ tsp garlic powder

½ tsp agave

½ tsp sea salt

1 tbsp (9 g) plus 1 tsp tapioca starch

White pepper, to taste

BUTTERMILK SAUCE

In a small pot, blanch the mallow buds for 2 to 3 minutes in lightly salted, boiling water. Remove the mallow buds from the water and place them in a bowl of cold water to stop the cooking process.

Discard the liquid and using the same pot, combine the buttermilk, apple cider vinegar, turmeric (if using), dill, chives, onion powder, garlic powder, agave and salt and bring to a simmer. Turn the heat down to medium and whisk in the tapioca starch 1 teaspoon at a time. Turn the heat to medium-low and cook, whisking for about 3 to 4 minutes until thickened. It should be the consistency of hot buttermilk dressing. Add the white pepper. Taste for saltiness and sweetness and adjust as needed. It should taste like the eponymous dressing.

To serve, spoon the sauce over the square pasta sheet, add half of the mallow buds, another layer of pasta, more buds and sauce to create beautiful, messy layers. I like to serve this with grated carrots and zucchini over the top.

Mallow Pappardelle

Pickled Mallow, Olives, Charred Grapes, Goat Feta and Pine Nuts over Pappardelle

Serves: 2 — Difficulty level: Easy

This dish is very easy to assemble. It takes advantage of the larger, less tender mallow leaves later in the season. They are pickled in the same way you would pickle grape leaves, and you want to select leaves approximately that size for this process.

PICKLED MALLOW

6 cups (1.4 L) water

3 tbsp (45 g) sea salt

8 cups (120 g) mallow leaves, washed and stemmed

3 tsp (14 g) citric acid

PASTA

1 cup (240 ml) water

1½ tbsp (23 g) sea salt

1½ cups (227 g) red globe grapes

7 oz (200 g) pappardelle pasta

2 tbsp (30 ml) olive oil

1 clove garlic, minced

¼ cup pitted green olives, chopped

1 tsp fresh oregano leaves, roughly chopped

1 tbsp (5 g) fresh parsley, roughly chopped

Red pepper flakes, to taste

2 cylinders pickled mallow leaves

4 oz (115 g) fresh goat feta

½ cup (63 g) toasted pine nuts, lightly crushed

To make the pickled mallow, in a large stockpot, bring the water and salt to a boil. Add the mallow leaves and boil for just under 2 minutes. Fish the leaves out carefully and place them into a bowl of ice water to cool down. The leaves will be delicate, so carefully stack them on top of one another as you would grape leaves—about 10 leaves high—and roll them into cigar-shaped cylinders. Place the cylinders in sterilized jars, but don't overcrowd them. You want enough room for the brine to cover everything. The mallow cylinders and brine should leave ½ inch (13 mm) of room from the top of the jar.

Meanwhile, to the same stockpot and water you just used to a boil the mallow, add the citric acid and bring the water back up to a boil again over high heat. Ladle the hot liquid over the mallow cylinders in the jars and secure the lids on the jars. You can keep the pickled mallow in the refrigerator for a few weeks.

To make the pasta, in a medium bowl, add the water to the salt. Once the salt has dissolved, roll the grapes in the solution until they are coated. Remove the grapes and place them on aluminum foil on a small baking sheet. Broil for 5 to 6 minutes or until the grapes are a little charred and split. Set aside.

In a large stockpot over high heat, bring salted water to a boil and prepare the pappardelle according the package's instructions for al dente, about 8 to 10 minutes. Drain the pappardelle and reserve ½ cup (120 ml) of the pasta water.

While the pasta is cooking, in a small saucepan over medium heat, add the olive oil, garlic, olives, oregano and parsley and cook until the garlic is fragrant, 2 to 3 minutes. Add the red pepper flakes. Take the saucepan off the heat and add the mixture to a small food processor, along with the reserved pasta water. Process until blended. It doesn't have to be really smooth. It will be a light dressing.

Toss this mixture with the drained pappardelle. To serve, arrange the pappardelle on a platter and layer with the pickled mallow leaves, charred grapes, crumbled feta and pine nuts. Finish with a few more red pepper flakes and a light drizzle of olive oil.

Plantain and Purslane *Poke*

Vegan Watermelon, Tomato and Plantain Poke

Serves: 2-4 — **Difficulty level:** Advanced

Although watermelon and tomato sushi have been around for a while, I thought turning it into a Hawaiian-style poke (which is traditionally raw, cubed, marinated tuna) dish might be fun. The young plantain leaves are my "wakame of the forest." They have a very similar texture, color and consistency to seaweed and even a faint sea smell when blanched. I had a blast making this dish the first time, because I served it to my spouse, whose favorite food is raw tuna. For a minute, he actually thought he was eating poke and seaweed.

1 (2-lb [910-g]) seedless watermelon

2 cups (480 ml) plus 1 tbsp (15 ml) olive oil

½ cup (120 ml) sake

1 tsp plus 2 pinches black or pink Hawaiian salt

4 tbsp (56 g) butter (or 2 tbsp [30 ml] olive oil for a vegan version)

2 large beefsteak tomatoes

4 cups (80 g) densely packed small, young plantain leaves, washed

2 tbsp (3 g) ogonori (a.k.a. ogo, a type of Hawaiian black wiry seaweed)

½ tsp sesame oil

1 tsp soy sauce (or tamari for a gluten-free version)

⅛ tsp red pepper flakes

1 tbsp (15 ml) rice wine vinegar

2 cups (86 g) purslane leaves, washed and stemmed

2 scallions, thinly sliced

1 tsp toasted sesame seeds

Preheat the oven to 300°F (149°C).

Cut the top and bottom off the watermelon, then cut the body of watermelon into 4 (1½-inch [4-cm] thick) slices. Cut off the rind from the slices, making the slices square. Oil the bottom of a small, shallow heat-proof dish with 1 tablespoon (15 ml) of the olive oil. Place the watermelon slices in the dish so they lie flat. Pour the sake over them evenly, sprinkle them with the pinch salt and dot them evenly with the butter (or drizzle on the olive oil if you are making a vegan version of this recipe). Cover the dish with aluminum foil and place the dish on a medium baking sheet. Bake the watermelon for 2 hours. Once the watermelon slices are cool enough to handle, drain them and pat dry. Slice them into sushi-like strips and set aside.

While the watermelon is baking, prepare the tomatoes. Add enough water to a medium stockpot to cover the tomatoes by 1 inch (3 cm). Cut an X in the bottom of each tomato and boil them for 3 to 4 minutes to loosen the skins. Remove the tomatoes from the water and let them cool down enough to handle. Remove the skins, then quarter the tomatoes and remove the seeds and membranes. Pat the tomatoes dry and add them to a small, shallow, heat-proof baking dish with the remaining pinch salt. Cover the tomatoes with the remaining 2 cups (480 ml) olive oil. Make sure the olive oil is just covering the tomatoes. Put the tomatoes in the oven for the watermelon's last 30 minutes of cooking. Remove them from the olive oil and pat them dry.

In a small pot over high heat, blanch the plantain leaves in lightly salted water for 3 minutes. Drain and place them in a small bowl of cold water to stop the cooking process. Remove the plantain leaves and set them aside until you are ready to assemble the salad, but do not drain the bowl. Soak the ogonori in the same bowl of water for 5 to 7 minutes. Drain the ogonori and set aside.

In a medium salad bowl, whisk together the sesame oil, soy sauce, the remaining 1 teaspoon salt, red pepper flakes, vinegar and ogonori. Add the watermelon slices, tomatoes, plantain leaves and purslane leaves, and toss gently. Top the salad with the scallions and toasted sesame seeds. Let the dish marinate for at least 20 minutes in the refrigerator and serve chilled. It goes well with cold sake.

Spicy Cattail and Chorizo Salsa

Cattail and Pineapple Salad with Quick Chorizo

Serves: 2-4 — Difficulty level: Easy

Cattail shoots have the benefit of cooling and soothing the tongue. I think that as far as flavor and texture go, cattail shoots are a cross between cucumber and aloe. There's a very slight mucilaginous quality. They have a natural affinity for spicy and sharp foods. I also love the combination of cattail and pineapple. To my palate, the combination is harmonious. The following isn't so much a recipe as a suggestion of flavor combinations.

4 tbsp (60 ml) olive oil, divided

3 cloves garlic, minced

½ lb (228 g) ground pork

½ tsp plus pinch sea salt, divided

½ tsp brown sugar

½ tsp California chili powder

½ tsp dried oregano

½ tsp ground cumin

⅛ tsp cayenne

½ tsp achiote powder (also called annatto), optional

2 tbsp (30 ml) fresh lime juice

1 medium red jalapeño (14 g), ribs and seeds removed, finely chopped

½ small red onion, cut into ¼-inch (6-mm) pieces

2 tbsp (10 g) roughly chopped fresh cilantro

8 oz (228 g) cattail shoots, washed and cut into ¼-inch (6-mm) pieces

1 medium pineapple, peeled, cored and cut into ½-inch (13-mm) cubes

In a medium sauté pan over medium-high heat, add 2 tablespoons (30 ml) of the oil. Add the garlic and sauté for 1 minute, until fragrant. Add the pork in chunks followed by ½ teaspoon of the salt and cook for 2 minutes, turning the pork and breaking it apart. Sprinkle the brown sugar, California chili powder, oregano, cumin, cayenne and achiote powder over the top and stir to combine well. Continue to cook until browned, 6 to 8 minutes. Drain the pork and set aside.

To a medium bowl, add the remaining 2 tablespoons (30 ml) oil, lime juice, jalapeño, onion, cilantro and cattail shoots. Add the pineapple and the pinch salt and toss. Let this marinate for at least 10 minutes.

Serve by layering the salsa and chorizo in a bowl. Some sour cream, corn chips and extra cilantro on the side would be welcome.

Oi Naengguk with
Cattail and Plantain

Serves: 4 — Difficulty level: Easy

I currently live close to a predominantly Korean neighborhood. I'm so lucky there are many great Korean markets and restaurants nearby. I happen to love Korean food and pretty much everything about it. I was inspired to make this dish not only because it was heat-wave hot outside, but also because I was out of so many basic things. This dish is traditionally based around cucumbers and seaweed. When I thought about it, I had some foraged things on hand that were perfect substitutes, namely cattail shoots and plantain. This dish is served as a cold soup, but I made it into a savory cocktail.

2 cups (40 g) densely packed plantain leaves, washed

3½ cups (840 ml) cold water

½ cup (120 ml) chilled soju or sake

1 tbsp (15 ml) tamari

2 tbsp (30 ml) seasoned rice wine vinegar

1 tsp agave

½ tsp sesame oil

1 scallion, finely chopped

1 red Indian or Thai chili or red jalapeño, minced

½ tsp toasted black sesame seeds

2 cattail shoots, finely sliced on the bias

Gochugaru (Korean chili flakes), as needed to rim the glasses

Ice, as needed

In a small pot of lightly salted water over high heat, blanch the plantain leaves for 3 minutes. Remove the leaves and plunge them in a bowl of cold water to stop the cooking process.

In a pitcher, combine the soju, tamari, vinegar, agave, oil, scallion, red Indian or Thai chili and sesame seeds, stirring to combine. Put the gochugaru on a plate or in a small bowl. Prep 4 glasses by dipping the rims in water and then into the gochugaru. Add one-fourth of the plantain leaves and one-fourth of the cattail shoots to each glass, along with enough ice to fill the glass halfway. In a bar shaker filled with ice, add half the pitcher of liquid and shake for at least 30 seconds. Fill 2 glasses, repeat the process and fill the remaining 2 glasses.

Cattail Pollen Madeleines

Butter, Vanilla and Cattail Pollen

Makes: about 24 mini cookies — **Difficulty level:** Moderate

I love the beautiful color of cattail pollen. It does have some nutritional value, as well—it's a source of iron and phosphorus and a very good source of dietary fiber, vitamin K, vitamin B$_6$, calcium, magnesium, potassium, manganese and antioxidants. The pollen itself doesn't have much of a flavor or aroma (except for a slightly floral, grassy smell), but the texture is remarkably like all-purpose flour. Many foragers add it to pancakes for a breakfast boost. But when I see cattail pollen in abundance, I immediately think of brightly colored, buttery madeleines. (Note: Using a nonstick madeleine pan is key, especially if you haven't baked these before. The key to successful madeleines is butter, butter, butter. This is a small batch adapted for mini cookies, but you can easily double the recipe if you are making medium- or standard-size madeleines.)

5 tbsp (70 g) butter, melted and cooled, divided

¼ cup (31 g) all-purpose flour, plus 1 tbsp (8 g) for flouring the pan

1 large egg

½ tsp pure vanilla extract

Pinch sea salt

⅓ cup (64 g) sugar

¼ cup (20 g) cattail pollen

Preheat the oven to 375°F (191°C). Chill your madeleine pan for at least 1 hour in the freezer before use.

Thoroughly brush the madeleine pan with 1 tablespoon (14 g) of the butter using a silicone brush or pastry brush. Make sure to get into every crevice and surface, including the top of the pan. It's also important to have an even layer and no excess dribbles or droplets of butter in the pan. Dust the top of the pan evenly with 1 tablespoon (8 g) of the flour, taking care to shake or tap out any excess flour, leaving no clumps. The clumps are what will prevent the madeleines from releasing from the pan, resulting in torn cookies.

In a food processor fitted with the dough blade, add the egg, vanilla, salt and sugar and blend until well combined (about 1 to 2 minutes). In a small bowl, combine the flour and pollen. Add the flour mixture to the processor and pulse until just combined. With the machine on low speed, slowly pour in the remaining 4 tablespoons (56 g) butter in an even stream until just combined. You can use a spatula to fold everything together.

Carefully pour the batter into each madeleine cup in the pan, filling each cup about three-fourths full.

Bake the mini madeleines for 10 to 12 minutes (or about 15 minutes for medium-size madeleines). Check on them after 10 minutes. Because of the butter content, they can burn easily. Tip them out of the pan onto a cooling rack. If they stick a bit, use a sharp paring knife to loosen them. Let them cool completely.

I like to serve these with a brushing of browned butter, a dusting of powdered sugar and some hot black tea with cream.

Abdoogh Khiar with *Cattail*

Kefir over Ice with Cattail, Fresh Herbs, Chives and Dried Fruit

Serves: 4 — Difficulty level: Easy

I was working outside in the heat, sweating up a storm, a few years ago when our lovely Persian-Armenian neighbors brought me this magical elixir in a bowl. Concerned about the redness of my face, they urged me to consume it immediately. I did and I felt cooler and instantly better. What they gave me was so simple and delicious. It was a yogurt "soup" with ice cubes, raisins, cucumber, mint, tarragon and scallions with a few pieces of *lavash* bread thrown in to soak. Sweet, savory and lactic but refreshing and clean. I loved their recipe as it was, but I have changed it up a bit—I think cattail shoots work in this dish so beautifully, and I like the rosehips for a bit of tartness in contrast with the sweet, floral mulberries.

1 lb (455 g) plain kefir or yogurt

½ tsp sea salt

4 tbsp (60 ml) ice water

¼ cup (20 g) fresh dill, finely chopped

1 tbsp (5 g) finely chopped fresh marjoram

1 tbsp (2 g) crushed dried rose petals

2 tbsp (10 g) finely chopped fresh chives

2 tbsp (6 g) finely chopped fresh mint

⅛ cup (16 g) dried rosehips, cleaned

⅛ cup (16 g) dried mulberries, roughly chopped

4 oz (115 g) cattail shoots, soaked per page 48, trimmed and cut on the diagonal crosswise

2 cups (280 g) ice

In a large bowl, combine the yogurt, salt and ice water and mix to thin out the yogurt. Add the dill, marjoram, rose petals, chives, mint, rosehips and mulberries and stir to combine. Fold in the cattail shoots. Serve in a big serving bowl, family-style, with 4 smaller bowls each filled with ½ cup (70 g) ice. I like to serve this with some toasted lavash strips and fresh split figs with honey on the side. With some sweet mint and nettle tea, this is a wonderful get-together feast on a hot afternoon.

Cattail Flower Seafood Boil

Cattail, Shrimp and Spices

Serves: 2 — Difficulty level: Easy

I think this is one of the first wild-food dishes I made because it made sense to me. There were also many crawfish and cattail flowers available at the time, and it just seemed perfect. This dish takes advantage of the flowering cattail heads or "cobs." You can eat both the female and male cobs, but there is a very specific window: too early and there's not a lot on the cob, too late and it's turned fibrous. I do not make this very often. It is more of a special-occasion dish when the cattails are especially invasive. The corn-like flavor of the cobs is mild and neutral and can take the heat and flavor of crab-boil seasoning. In addition, it is another use for harvested mustard seeds.

SPICE SACHET

½ tsp coriander seeds

3–4 allspice berries

2–3 whole cloves

1 large dried bay leaf

¼ tsp dill seeds

1 tsp mustard seeds

CRAB BOIL

4½ cups (1.1 L) water

1 tsp plus pinch sea salt

1 clove garlic, smashed

Pinch cayenne

½ lemon, quartered

1 small onion, peeled and quartered

4 small red potatoes, washed and quartered

2 cattail cobs, trimmed and cut in two

6 jumbo shell-on shrimp (6 oz [170 g]), deveined and cleaned

To make the spice sachet, combine the coriander seeds, allspice berries, cloves, bay leaf, dill seeds and mustard seeds in a spice bag or a piece of cheesecloth that can be formed into a purse with kitchen twine.

In a small pot over high heat, bring the water to a rolling boil and add the salt and spice sachet. Let this boil for 10 minutes. Add the garlic, cayenne, lemon, onion and potatoes and cook for 10 to 12 more minutes. Pierce the centers of the potatoes to see if they are tender. If so, remove the potatoes, set aside and add the cattail cobs and shrimp. Cook for 7 to 8 more minutes, then remove the cobs and shrimp and set aside with the potatoes. Taste the broth for seasoning and adjust if needed.

Ladle the broth into 2 soup bowls and add half the potatoes, shrimp, cattail cobs and onion to each bowl. Serve with some garlic and herb dirty rice and a salad.

Field "Wakame" and Clams

Clams and Plantain with Sake

Serves: 2 — Difficulty level: Easy

This is another easy dish for entertaining. It takes no time to prepare and has few ingredients. The texture of the young plantain leaves mimics tender seaweed, or wakame, and pairs well with the brininess of the clams and aromatic sake.

1 tbsp (15 ml) olive oil

1 small leek, cleaned and sliced into ¼-inch (6-mm) thick circles

¼ cup (24 g) 1-inch (3-cm) thick slices fresh ginger

1 tsp sea salt, divided

2 cloves garlic, minced

3 cups (720 ml) water

1 cup (240 ml) dry sake

2 lb (500 g) littleneck clams or other sweet or local variety

6 cups (120 g) densely packed small, young plantain leaves, washed

In a medium stockpot over medium heat, add the oil, leek, ginger and ½ teaspoon of the salt and cook for 5 to 6 minutes or until the leek is tender. Add the garlic and cook 1 more minute. Add the water and sake and simmer for 15 minutes. Taste the broth for seasoning and add the remaining ½ teaspoon salt if needed. Add the clams and plantain leaves and cook covered for 5 to 6 minutes or until the clams have opened. Remove any dead or unopened clams and serve in large bowls with a few roasted wild onions if you have them available.

Chapter Four

Earthy and Spicy Brassica

Mustard and Radish

He saw the kind of beauty yellow flowers have growing over a carpet of dead leaves. The beauty of cracks forming a mosaic in a dry riverbed, of emerald-green algae at the base of a seawall, of a broken shard from a blue bottle. The beauty of a window smudged with tiny prints. The beauty of wild weeds.

– Michelle Cuevas, *Beyond the Laughing Sky*

Mustard

Brassicaceae family

Brassica is introduced and present in every US state and most of Canada, as well as worldwide

Invasive

The two most common mustards in North America are: *Brassica nigra* (black mustard) and *Hirschfeldia incana* (hoary or Mediterranean mustard), formerly Brassica geniculata both are closely related and edible as a vegetable (the leaves, seeds and flowers).

Flavor Profile

The striking difference between these two plants is the flavor. Black mustard tastes, well, like spicy mustard. The seeds, leaves, buds and flowers are pungent and spicy. For this reason, I use this species in most raw applications as the spiciness fades away with cooking. The only thing to mention about *Hirschfeldia incana* is that the flowers are great for garnish and the leaves suitable for cooking. They both have a cabbage-like or broccoli-like flavor. Leaves, buds and some roots have a musty, earthy cruciferous essence and the seeds of some mustard species have a wasabi-like, hot mustard punch.

Mustard leaves (*Hirschfeldia incana*)

Black mustard flowers (*Brassica nigra*)

Black mustard field (*Brassica nigra*)

Current Known Range

When and How to Harvest

Mustard blankets the hills, fields, roadsides and trails where I live and starts to appear in midspring to early summer. Later in the season, as the weather becomes hot and dry, the plants lose their blossoms, dry out and become brown, which means it's time to gather the seeds. I find this plant growing in a variety of soil conditions, from sandy and loamy to fertile and moist. This plant loves direct sunlight but can also be found in some semi-shaded, dappled areas. It is pretty indestructible. This is quite an easy one to spot if it grows in your area. Because the seeds are tiny and disperse in wide areas, they create large pockets or fields of bright yellow blossoms that can grow anywhere from 3 to 6 feet (1 to 2 m) tall.

Distinguishing Identifiers

- Bright yellow flowers with four petals (two long, two short) and six stamens

- Shiny but bumpy alligator-like leaves

- Distinct mustard smell when crushed (like wasabi)

- Seed pods split open to reveal a clear membrane with the seeds inside

- With *Hirschfeldia incana*, the seeds are not black but a golden color and the leaves are often smaller and have a fine coat of little hairs (they are still great for cooking, and I'll use them for stewing or baking)

Possible Look-Alikes

- *Raphanus* or field radish when not flowering (mustard and radish will often grow together or near each other)

Radish

Raphanus raphanistrum (wild radish),
Raphanus sativus (cultivated radish),
Raphanus caudatus (rattail radish)

Brassicaceae family

Invasive

Flavor Profile

The rattail radish pods are crunchy, juicy and crisp before they toughen and seed. They deliver quite a spicy punch not unlike horseradish and are a fantastic addition in salads. The leaves of all species of radish are nice, mild, earthy cooking greens. I use the young buds before they flower as a broccoli substitute and also dry and pickle the tender stems of the radish plant.

When and How to Harvest

Like mustard, radishes take over entire fields as far as the eye can see with small flowers that range from pastel yellow and lavenders to bright purples and magentas. You can find them in pastures, roadsides and along trails as well. It's like walking through a salad with their sharp radish smell. The radishes like a bit more shade and water than mustard, and I often find the

Wild Radish Range

Current Known Range

Wild radish flowers (*R. raphanistrum*)

Rattail radish pods (*Raphanus caudatus*)

Cultivated Radish Range

Current Known Range

best ones under a canopy of trees near a wash. Harvest the leaves toward the middle and top of the plant and the flowers sparingly. There's a small window of time to harvest the pods before they harden.

Distinguishing Identifiers

- Single pastel four-petal flowers (white, yellow, purple)

- Tiny, pale green radish pods

- Radish-like smell when crushed

- Smaller/shorter plant than mustard

Possible Look-Alikes

- Wild arugula (if flowering) and mustard (if not flowering)

Wild Radish Leaf Ribollita

Wild Radish Leaf and Summer Vegetable Stew with Beans over Toasted Bread

Serves: 4 — Difficulty level: Easy

You cannot get more basic than this dish in terms of simplicity and frugality. It is a great summer dish because the mustard leaves are abundant at the same time as the herbs in the garden as well as summer tomatoes. Traditional recipes call for tinned tomatoes, but I use fresh here. Even though the stale bread is an integral part of this dish, I often enjoy the soup with farro. What pairs well with the earthiness of the mustard is the unbelievable velvety quality of the gigante beans—and they are giant! While not Italian, these Greek beans are the king of beans to me. You can find them dry, but they can be a little difficult to cook and you can find canned gigantes of excellent quality. True to form, they usually come in a giant 70-ounce (2 kg) can, but this is something you'll be glad you purchased and will use in many dishes.

6 cups (1.4 L) water

5 medium tomatoes, divided

6 cups (228 g) radish leaves, washed and stemmed

3 small leeks, cleaned and finely chopped

1 medium celery stalk, thinly sliced

½ medium carrot, thinly sliced

1 tsp dried oregano

1 tsp sea salt, divided

3 cloves garlic, sliced

¼ cup (60 ml) white wine

1 dried bay leaf

8 oz (227 g) canned gigante beans, drained

8 (½-inch [13-mm] thick) slices French bread, toasted

2 tbsp (10 g) finely chopped fresh basil

2 tbsp (10 g) roughly chopped fresh parsley

4 tsp (20 ml) good-quality balsamic vinegar

Bring the water to a boil in a medium stockpot over high heat. Make an X on the bottom of 4 tomatoes with a sharp knife and blanch them for 3 to 4 minutes in the boiling water. Remove the tomatoes carefully and set aside to cool slightly. When they are cool enough to handle but still hot, peel the skins off. Quarter the peeled tomatoes and remove and discard the seeds. Set the flesh aside. Reserve the tomato cooking water in the stockpot.

In a medium sauté pan over medium heat, add the radish leaves, leeks, celery, carrot, oregano and ½ teaspoon of the salt. Cook for 5 to 7 minutes until the vegetables are soft. Add the garlic and cook for another 1 to 2 minutes until fragrant. Add the wine and reduce it by one-third, about 5 to 7 minutes. Transfer the vegetable mixture to the pot of tomato water with the blanched quartered tomatoes, beans, bay leaf and the remaining ½ teaspoon salt. Bring the soup it to a simmer over medium-high heat and cook, covered, for 20 minutes, stirring once or twice.

While the soup is cooking, chop the remaining tomato into ½-inch (13-mm) cubes. Set aside.

To serve, place 2 slices French bread in the bottom of each of 4 bowls, ladle the soup over the bread and garnish with the basil, fresh tomato, parsley and a drizzle of the balsamic vinegar.

*See picture on page 74.

Black on Black *Radish* Greens

Charred Radish Greens with Garlic and Squid Ink Pasta

Serves: 4 — Difficulty level: Easy

This dish was inspired by a neighbor and friend. In fact, she was my very first friend and neighbor in Los Angeles when I moved here. It was something her mother often made in a pinch. It's a simple dish of spaghetti and pan-charred cabbage with lots of garlic and Parmesan. The toasty, almost charred flavor of the cabbage just about made the dish. I still love this dish and if I get home late and am starving, it's definitely my go-to. I've updated it here with wild radish greens, which have that same musty, earthy flavor profile. The squid ink pasta is not only beautiful but it also lends a hidden umami quality.

1 (17.6-oz [500-g]) package squid ink spaghetti

2 tbsp (30 ml) olive oil

6 cups (228 g) radish leaves, washed, trimmed and roughly chopped

2 tbsp (14 g) butter

4 cloves garlic, minced

Pinch sea salt

2 tbsp (6 g) roughly chopped fresh oregano, plus a few sprigs for garnish

¼ cup (60 ml) dry white wine

6 tbsp (30 g) shaved Parmesan, divided

Freshly ground black pepper, to taste

In a large stockpot, prepare the spaghetti according to the package's directions (typically in rapidly boiling salted water for 7 to 10 minutes). Drain, reserving 4 to 5 tablespoons (60 to 75 ml) of the pasta water.

While the spaghetti is cooking, heat the oil in a large sauté pan over medium-high heat. Add the radish leaves and cook for about 4 minutes or until they get a nice char on one side. Turn the heat down to medium and add the butter, garlic, salt, oregano, wine, reserved pasta water and 1 tablespoon (5 g) of the Parmesan and toss to cook the other side of the radish leaves for another 3 minutes, letting the wine reduce a bit. Turn off the heat, add the cooked spaghetti and toss, coating and combining the pasta and radish leaves thoroughly. Taste for seasoning and adjust as needed. Serve the spaghetti family-style and garnish with the remaining 5 tablespoons (25 g) Parmesan, oregano sprigs and freshly ground black pepper.

The *Wild* Rabbit

Mugwort Beer Rarebit and Mustard Greens

Serves: 4-6 — Difficulty level: Advanced

This recipe, which is actually several recipes in one, is a take on Welsh rarebit or "rabbit." I actually thought of it because I saw rabbits eating the field mustard. True story. And my spouse makes home-brewed beer. The thought of earthy greens, sharp cheddar and beer all melty and delicious made me a little giddy. This is an excellent introduction to mustard greens for people who may not eat weeds that often.

This recipe gets a lot of its flavor from mustard seeds, as well. We also make our own mustard with the mustard seeds. Where we live, there are literally acres and acres of mustard fields, both black and Mediterranean. We collect enough seeds to make a few jars of our own mustard every year. This prepared mustard is adapted from *The New Wildcrafted Cuisine: Exploring the Exotic Gastronomy of Local Terroir* by Pascal Baudar.

I like using sourdough or fermented dough in any baking recipe if I can, and that includes the crust for this dish. It is easy to make a sourdough starter and there are many recipes online. They are all simple and involve sugar, flour, yeast, water and a little time. It's worth investigating.

PIE CRUST

2 cups (250 g) all-purpose flour

1 tbsp (12 g) sugar

1 tsp sea salt

1½ cups (345 g) cold butter or lard, cubed

1 cup (240 ml) sourdough starter

PREPARED MUSTARD

½ cup (120 ml) champagne vinegar

⅓ cup (80 ml) dry white wine

2 tsp (10 ml) honey

⅓ cup (5 g) black mustard seeds

1½ tsp (8 g) sea salt

PIE CRUST

In a food processor fitted with the dough blade, add the flour, sugar and salt and blend for 1 minute to sift and combine. Add the butter, ½ cup (115 g) at a time, pulsing the machine between each addition. You want to see pea-size butter pieces distributed throughout. Gradually pour in the sourdough starter and pulse until combined. Transfer the dough to a bowl and cover it with plastic wrap. Let the dough sit out 8 to 10 hours or up to overnight. The next morning, form the dough into a ball, wrap it in plastic wrap and transfer it to the refrigerator to chill for at least 2 hours.

PREPARED MUSTARD

In a medium measuring cup, combine the vinegar, wine and honey. To a small food processor, add the mustard seeds and salt. Slowly add one-quarter of the vinegar mixture to the processor and process for 5 minutes, then let the processor rest 5 minutes. Repeat this process until all the vinegar mixture is incorporated into the mustard mixture. Taste the mustard for salt, adjusting if needed, and then transfer it to a glass jar with a tight-fitting lid. Let the mustard age in the refrigerator for 2 to 3 days before using to mellow the bitterness. Stir before using.

RAREBIT SAUCE

2 tbsp (28 g) cold butter

2 tbsp (16 g) all-purpose flour

½ cup (120 ml) stout beer

½ cup (120 ml) heavy cream

2 tsp (10 g) Prepared Mustard

⅛ tsp smoked paprika

⅛ tsp onion powder

1½ cups (181 g) shredded sharp Cheddar

1 large egg yolk

4 cups (120 g) mustard leaves, washed, stemmed and finely chopped

RAREBIT SAUCE

Preheat the oven to 375°F (191°C).

In a medium stockpot over medium heat, melt the butter and whisk in the flour until well combined. Whisk in the beer, then the cream and then the mustard, smoked paprika and onion powder. The mixture may foam up a bit and separate, but keep whisking vigorously and bring the mixture to barely a simmer to cook out the raw flour and cream flavors. The mixture will come back together. Whisk in the cheese until melted.

In a small bowl, beat the egg yolk and temper it by ladling in 1 teaspoon at a time of the hot cheese mixture, whisking continuously. You'll probably have to add 5 to 6 teaspoons (25 to 30 ml) to bring the egg yolk to a temperature that will prevent it from scrambling when you add it to the pot. Once you have added the tempered egg yolk to the pot, whisk and cook for another 3 to 4 minutes. Add the mustard leaves and cook for another 5 minutes. Turn off the heat and let the mixture cool.

Just before baking, roll the pie crust out to about ⅛ inch (3 mm) thick and large enough to fit a standard 9-inch (23-cm) pie pan. Prick the bottom crust all over with a fork. Pour the cheesy mixture into the prepared crust and bake for 20 minutes or until the edges of the pie crusts are browned. The recipe makes about 2½ cups (592 ml) of cheese sauce.

Rarebit and mustard greens

Harvested mustard seeds

Pan-Seared Mustard or Radish Leaves

Blistered Greens with Mix-and-Match Seasonings

Serves 2-4 — Difficulty level: Easy

The reason I am including this recipe is twofold. Every time I make this while teaching a class or just for friends and family, almost everyone says it's one of their favorite new ways to eat harvested mustard and radish leaves and they can't believe they didn't think of it before. It's like kale chips or chips made from other greens, but way simpler. It's also adaptable to almost any type of cuisine (Asian, Mediterranean, European, American and so on).

SWEET HEAT

1 tbsp (15 ml) peanut oil

⅛ tsp cayenne

⅛ tsp brown sugar

Pinch sea salt

1 tbsp (25 g) crushed sweet potato chips, to dust over the top

SESAME YUZU

2¼ tsp (11 ml) vegetable oil

¼ tsp sesame oil

½ tsp yuzu or ponzu sauce

Pinch sea salt

1 tsp toasted sesame seeds

GREEK-STYLE

1 tbsp (15 ml) garlic-infused olive oil

1 tsp lemon-pepper salt with dried oregano

Heat a large cast iron pan over high heat. Lightly brush a flavored oil on one side of a leaf, lightly salt it and place it in cast iron pan until it blisters, about 1 minute. Turn the leaf and blister the other side. That's it. How you flavor it is entirely up to you. Here are some ideas. Mix these together and brush on 8 to 10 washed mustard or radish leaves.

Peixada with *Wild Mustard* Greens

Pumpkin, Coconut Milk and Mustard Greens Stew with Fish

Serves: 4-6 — Difficulty level: Easy

A *peixada* is a simple, Brazilian-style fish stew made with coconut milk and a mixture of vegetables. I love the addition of mustard greens to this dish because the earthy greens complement the slight sweetness of the coconut milk and pumpkin. This is a one-pot meal, but you can also roast off smaller pumpkins, hollow them out, and serve the stew inside. This dish is fragrant and satisfying but light as well.

2 tbsp (30 ml) olive or vegetable oil

1 large onion, cut into ½-inch (13-mm) pieces

1 medium green bell pepper, cored, seeded and cut into ½-inch (13-mm) pieces

Sea salt and white pepper, to taste

1 tsp sweet paprika or ½ tsp annatto seed oil

2 cloves garlic, minced

4 cups (960 ml) coconut cream

4 cups (960 ml) coconut milk

4 cups (464 g) pumpkin, peeled and cut into ½-inch (13-mm) cubes

6 cups (180 g) mustard leaves, washed, stemmed and roughly chopped

4 medium tomatoes, quartered

8 oz (228 g) fresh cod or other firm white fish, cut into 1-inch (3-cm) cubes

4 scallions, thinly sliced, for garnish

Fresh cilantro, for garnish

¼ cup (20 g) toasted coconut flakes, for garnish

In a heavy-bottomed medium stockpot over medium heat, add the oil, onion, bell pepper and a pinch of salt and sauté until the onions are soft, about 6 to 7 minutes. Add the paprika and garlic and cook for another 2 minutes, combining everything well. Add the coconut cream, coconut milk, pumpkin, mustard leaves and tomatoes and stir to combine. Season with salt and white pepper and bring up to a boil, then lower the heat to medium-low and bring the soup to a light simmer. Cover and cook for 25 minutes. The pumpkin should start to get a little tender. Add the cod, reduce the heat to low and cook for another 12 to 15 minutes.

To serve, ladle the soup into large bowls or serve in individual roasted pumpkins. Garnish the soup with the scallions, cilantro and toasted coconut. I sometimes serve this with a side of coconut rice.

Honey Duck and *Wild* Greens

Seared Duck with Buckwheat Honey, Black Beans and Radish Greens

Serves: 4 — Difficulty level: Easy

This is an impressive and impressively easy dish to do. It's good for both entertaining and everyday dinners.
The richness of the duck and sweet nuttiness of the beans are a great match for the slightly pungent greens.

1 cup (201 g) dried black soybeans

1½ tbsp (23 ml) Worcestershire sauce

½ tsp sea salt

2 tbsp (30 ml) dry white wine or sherry

1 tbsp (12 g) sugar

8 cups (304 g) radish leaves, washed, stemmed and roughly chopped

2 tbsp (30 ml) black buckwheat honey

4 (1-lb [455-g]) skin-on duck breasts

1 tbsp (15 g) flaked sea salt

4 scallions, finely chopped, for garnish

In a medium pot, soak the soybeans for at least 4 hours or up to overnight in cold water. Drain and rinse the beans. In the same pot over medium-high heat, cover the beans with 2 cups (480 ml) water and cook at a simmer for 5 to 7 minutes. Add the Worcestershire, salt, wine and sugar and cook for another 30 minutes. Add the radish leaves during the last 10 minutes of cooking, stirring occasionally so the greens and beans do not stick to the bottom of the pot. Most of the liquid should evaporate. Add the honey to coat and warm through. Taste for salt and adjust if needed. Keep the beans warm and set aside.

Preheat the oven to 400°F (204°C).

Pat the duck breasts dry with a paper towel and salt them generously (especially the skin) with the flaked salt. Place the duck breasts, skin-side down, in a large, cold sauté pan or cast iron pan with no oil. Make sure your pan is ovenproof with no plastic. Turn on the heat to medium-high and let the duck skin sear and render the fat for 7 to 8 minutes or until the breasts release easily and are browned. (I use a plate as a weight on top of the breasts to get an even sear.) Flip the breasts and cook for another 1 to 2 minutes. Transfer the pan to the oven, skin-side up, and finish cooking the breasts to medium rare, 6 to 7 minutes. The internal temperature for medium rare should be 135°F (57°C). Let the breasts rest for at least 10 minutes before slicing.

Serve on a platter, with the sliced duck arranged on a bed of the beans and greens. Scatter the scallions over the top.

Note: I've used Worcestershire sauce here, but you can substitute soy sauce or tamari if you want to make this gluten-free. When I make this, I actually use the brine from pickled green walnuts we harvest. It has the same rich, dark color as soy or Worcestershire sauce and a salty, tangy bite.

The Russian *Radish*

Sweet and Sour Quince with Radish and Mustard Greens Stew

Serves: 4 — Difficulty level: Easy

I love a good borscht and this one is slightly lighter and takes advantage of summer quince, which are ripe around the same time the mustard and radish greens are in full swing. You can use any economical cuts of meat, from oxtail to short ribs. This is my take on a Russian sweet and sour cabbage stew.

2 tbsp (30 ml) olive oil, divided

2 lb (910 g) cubed beef stew meat, cut into 2–3-inch (5–8-cm) pieces

1 medium onion, cut into ¼-inch (6-mm) pieces

4 cloves garlic, minced

6 oz (170 g) tomato paste

2 dried bay leaves

1 tsp sea salt

1 tsp freshly ground black pepper

¼ cup (60 ml) apple cider vinegar

2 large potatoes, peeled and cut into ½-inch (13-mm) cubes

2 large quince fruit, unpeeled, cored and quartered

8 cups (304 g) radish or mustard leaves (or a combination of both), washed, stemmed and roughly chopped

In a medium heavy-bottomed stockpot over high heat, add 1 tablespoon (15 ml) of the oil and sear the stew meat to a dark brown on all sides, about 7 to 10 minutes. Remove the meat and set aside. Turn down the heat to medium-high, add the remaining oil and cook the onion until soft, 5 to 6 minutes. Add the garlic and cook 1 more minute. Add the tomato paste, stirring to combine, and cook for another 3 to 4 minutes. Add the meat, bay leaves, salt, pepper, vinegar, potatoes, quince and radish leaves and cover the ingredients with water by about 1 inch (3 cm). Bring the stew to a boil over high heat, then reduce the heat to medium and bring the stew to a low simmer, with the lid slightly ajar, for 1 hour. Remove the lid and cook for another 30 minutes. Check the quince. It will hold its shape but it should be tender.

Serve with some crusty Russian country bread and sour cream.

Mustard "Moccolini"

Wild Mustard Buds with Almonds and Sultanas

Serves: 2 — Difficulty level: Easy

Just before the mustard plants flower, they form little clusters of green buds that look like tiny rapini, or broccoli rabe, clusters. They pretty much taste the same, too. This is a quick trail snack and a fun, tiny appetizer or starter. With a quick sauce of garlic, sultanas and almonds and a little wine, it's easy.

2 cups (80 g) mustard flower buds, washed and trimmed

2 tbsp (30 ml) olive oil

2 cloves garlic, thinly sliced

¼ cup (38 g) sultanas

¼ cup (21 g) slivered almonds, toasted

1 tbsp (15 ml) dry white wine

Pinch sea salt

Freshly ground black pepper, to taste

Blanch the mustard flower bud clusters in rapidly boiling salted water for 2 to 3 minutes. Drain and set aside. Heat the oil in a medium sauté pan over medium heat. Add the garlic and cook until slightly brown, about 1 to 2 minutes. Remove the garlic from the pan and set aside. Add the mustard flower buds, sultanas and almonds to the pan and sauté until everything is coated with the garlicky oil. Add the wine and salt and toss to combine. Cook for another 3 to 4 minutes until the wine has reduced and evaporated. Season with the pepper. Garnish with the garlic slices.

Mustard flower buds (*Brassica nigra*)

Ingredients for Mustard "Moccolini"

Puchero Asado Amarillo

Rare Steak with Spicy Mustard Flower Sauce

Serves: 2 — Difficulty level: Easy

This dish speaks to my Argentine roots and is very much like a typical Sunday night smashup dinner of *asado* and *puchero*, the former being an outdoor barbecue meat-fest and the other being a country stew of meat and usually root vegetables served with oil, vinegar and mustard. That's how we serve it in my family, at least.

In addition to making mustard from the actual seeds, many foragers make it from the flowers. While beautiful with all types of field mustard, it's uniquely delicious with black mustard (*Brassica nigra*) because of the wasabi-like bite and aroma. It reminds me of young horseradish. Mediterranean or other common field mustards will taste like broccoli.

1 cup (40 g) mustard flower leaves

¼ cup (60 ml) white wine

¼ cup (60 ml) champagne vinegar

½ tsp sea salt

1 clove garlic, minced

¼ tsp sugar

8 medium thin-skinned potatoes, washed and halved

8 small carrots, peeled

1 tbsp (14 g) butter, melted

4 tbsp (60 ml) olive oil, divided

2 tbsp (30 g) plus 1 tsp coarse Celtic salt, divided

2 (2-inch [6-cm]) thick T-bone steaks (about 2 lb [910 g] total)

8 large Pan-Seared Mustard or Radish Leaves (page 85), for garnish

With a small personal blender or an immersion blender with a cup attachment, pulse the mustard flowers, wine, vinegar, ½ teaspoon salt, 1 clove of the minced garlic and sugar until combined. I like to leave a few chunks of flowers and reserve a few flowers for garnish. Transfer this mixture to a serving dish and chill until ready to serve. Stir before serving.

Preheat a medium cast iron grill pan over high heat.

In a medium stockpot over high heat, boil the potatoes in salted water for 6 minutes. Add the carrots and cook for another 5 minutes. Check for doneness—the potatoes should be tender in the center and the carrots should not be cooked through all the way but should retain a hint of crunch. Drain the potatoes and carrots and toss them in a bowl with the butter and 1 tablespoon (15 ml) of the oil and ½ teaspoon of the Celtic salt and then sear them on the already hot grill pan to mark them.

Prepare the T-bone steaks by coating them thoroughly with 2 tablespoons (30 ml) of the oil and sprinkling the 2 tablespoons (30 g) Celtic salt on all sides of the steaks. When the grill pan is smoking, sear the steaks for 5 minutes on each side for rare. Stand the steaks up and grill the bones and fat, too. The internal temperature should reach 125°F (52°C). Immediately tent the meat with aluminum foil on a plate and let it rest for at least 15 minutes. It will continue to cook with the carry-over heat.

I like to serve this dish family-style, off the bone and thickly sliced, topped with the remaining ½ teaspoon Celtic salt and the remaining 1 tablespoon (15 ml) oil. Spoon plenty of the mustard flower mixture over the meat and vegetables and garnish with the mustard leaves.

Chapter Five

The Verdant And Herbaceous Nettle

It Doesn't Taste Like Spinach

When the nettle is young, the leaves make excellent greens; when it grows old it has filaments and fibers like hemp and flax. Cloth made from the nettle is worth as much as that made from hemp. Chopped up, the nettle is good for poultry; pounded, it is good for horned cattle. The seed of the nettle mixed with the fodder of animals gives a luster to their skin; the root, mixed with salt, produces a beautiful yellow dye. It makes, moreover, excellent hay, as it can be cut twice in a season. And what does the nettle need? Very little soil, no care, no culture; except that the seeds fall as fast as they ripen, and it is difficult to gather them; that is all. If we would take a little pains, the nettle would be useful; we neglect it, and it becomes harmful. Then we kill it. How much men are like the nettle! . . . My friends, remember this, that there are no bad herbs, and no bad men; there are only bad cultivators.

– Victor Hugo

Stinging Nettle

Urtica dioica

Urticaceae family

Native to North America, Europe,
Asia and Africa with a similar species
in Australia; spreads aggressively

Grows in shady, wooded areas where the
soil retains some moisture

Flavor Profile

I find the nettle to be not only a versatile plant to work with but also one with the most distinct flavor. There's really nothing that tastes exactly like it that you can find at your grocery store or market. In fact, the Urticaceae family is its very own family, so there really is nothing like it. A lot of people like to say it tastes like spinach, but I don't find that to be true for me. It has a slight herbal and very verdant quality while staying neutral and mild. It also stays vividly green during any type of cooking process and freezes well after blanching.

Another bonus is that, unlike other plants, it is not usually bitter even after it goes to flower and seed and the blanching liquid can be used for tea whereas the blanching liquid of other plants is very bitter and contains the oxalic acid or tannins you want to extract. There is some debate as to consuming nettles after they flower because it may cause kidney stones, but I've seen information that supports and contradicts this with nothing conclusive. Blanching the plant and using in moderation after it flowers is key.

Note: When blanching nettles or making teas or broths, use a nonreactive pot (ceramic ware or nonstick) and a wooden spoon. If you use reactive cookware (stainless or aluminum), your cooking liquid will oxidize and turn black, which is not always attractive.

Stinging nettle (*Urtica diotica*)

I adore nettles, as do specific kinds of bees, and I can't think of a reason not to plant it in your own garden or property. This is one plant that I would eat or drink every day if I could.

When and How to Harvest

Stinging nettles are available, depending on your region, throughout winter, spring and early summer, before they flower, go to seed and get a little tougher and less flavorful. In hotter climates, where I am, for example, the nettle season is pretty much done by early spring, but in cooler climates, you could see them throughout the summer.

Young nettles on forest floor (*Urtica diotica*)

You really want to treat foraging as you would pruning because it is essentially the same thing. Clip the side stems where they join the main base stem, alternating around the plant. You are actually promoting and controlling growth by taking only a small percentage (5 to 10 percent, depending on the size) of each plant. The way you harvest can actually increase the yield of the plant for future use. And it goes without saying that you shouldn't rip the plant out by the roots.

Distinguishing Identifiers

- Deltoid-shaped, jagged or toothy, veined, alternating leaves
- Stems are square in the cross section (similar to the mint family)
- Fine little hairs along the leaves and stems
- With older nettle plants, the stems can turn a reddish color

Possible Look-Alikes

- Young snakeroot
- Clearweed
- Horse-balm
- Wood nettle
- False nettle
- Dead nettle
- Germander

I use the leaves, mainly, unless I'm dehydrating them for tea, in which case I'll use the leaves and stems. The seeds are also edible and can be collected in late summer and fall to be used as a grain, much like lambsquarters seeds and amaranth seeds.

Like other foragers who know all too well the itchy, stingy but temporary tingle that comes with gathering nettles, I use a leather work glove, tongs and scissors or pruners. It's important not to pinch off or tear the plant when gathering because you can introduce disease into the plant, whereas the sharp scissors or pruners make a clean, healable break from the plant.

Note: Keep in mind that that you may have different species of nettle in your area. Not all plants with the common name "nettle" are edible. Again, it's important to do some classes with actual people to gain that confidence and knowledge as an oral tradition.

Nettle Canederli in Nettle Butter with Wild Mushrooms

Nettle and Potato Dumplings with Nettle Butter and Wild Mushrooms

Serves: 4-6 — Difficulty level: Moderate

Canederli are Tyrolean-style, potato based dumplings very similar to the German *kartoffelkloesse*, Bavarian *semmelknödel* or Austrian *knödel*. It even reminds me of matzo balls. I'm sure many cultures have a variation of them as they are made from very simple and humble ingredients, like potatoes and stale bread, and these dumplings can make a meal from very little. I develop intense cravings for them every once in a while and I consider this extreme comfort food. The reason I love to make these with nettles is that they provide just the right amount of bright green herbaceousness to the fluffy potato balls—and with the addition of nettle-infused butter spooned over them . . . well, oh my.

These canederli are extremely versatile and you can use the base recipe for any number of variations. It's a riced potato mixed with potato flour and cake flour and formed around a buttered bread cube, but feel free to use a cube of meat, cheese or whatever your heart desires.

This dish does take time, but the ingredients are very basic. If done right, canederli are fluffy and light and slightly spongey. If not mixed properly, though, they are disappointing, dense and bland balls of potato. I have made both versions, so hopefully this recipe will work out beautifully for you.

1 cup (25 g) dried porcini mushrooms

2 cups (25 g) dried, flaked oyster mushrooms

2 large potatoes, washed

4 cups (60 g) densely packed nettle leaves, washed and stemmed, divided

¾ cup (172 g) butter, divided

1 tbsp (15 ml) olive oil

1 clove garlic, finely minced

2 slices rustic sourdough bread, cut into about 16 cubes

1 tsp plus pinch sea salt, divided

Freshly ground black pepper, to taste

2 tbsp (10 g) fresh chervil or 1 tsp dried thyme or oregano

½ cup (50 g) cake flour

⅛ tsp ground nutmeg

⅛ cup (21 g) potato starch

1 large egg, beaten

1 tsp sea salt

Let the porcini mushrooms and oyster mushrooms rehydrate in 2½ cups (600 ml) hot water for at least 1 hour. Strain the mushrooms from the water and set them aside, but do not discard the liquid—just make sure any sand or debris that may have been in the mushrooms is strained out. Set the strained mushroom water aside.

Boil the potatoes in a large stockpot of moderately salted water over high heat for about 20 to 25 minutes. Start checking the potatoes after 18 minutes and pierce one with a sharp knife to see if the center gives. Once the potatoes are thoroughly cooked, drain them and let them cool until you can handle them. You should be able to peel the skins away and discard them.

(continued)

When the potatoes are completely cool, mash them through a potato ricer for the lightest and fluffiest results. Tip: Rice them over a baking sheet lined with parchment paper. This will require less handling than mixing them in a bowl.

In a medium stockpot over high heat, blanch the nettle leaves for 2 to 3 minutes in salted water. Drain them and when they are cool enough to handle, wring them slightly in a clean kitchen towel, finely chop and set aside.

Meanwhile, preheat the oven to 350°F (177°C). Melt ¼ cup (57 g) of the butter with the oil in an oven-safe medium sauté pan over medium heat and add the garlic and cook until the garlic is just fragrant, about 1 minute. Take the pan off the heat and add the bread cubes, tossing to coat them with the butter and garlic and toast them in the oven for 5 to 7 minutes or until golden brown. Remove from oven and let cool.

Using the same sauté pan, melt the remaining ½ cup (115 g) butter. Add 1 cup (15 g) of the finely chopped nettle leaves and the rehydrated mushrooms. If you are using dried herbs, add them now along with the garlic. Let the mixture cook over low heat for 2 to 3 minutes. Add the pinch salt and season with the pepper. Keep the butter warm. Add the chervil (if using) to the warm butter right before serving.

In a small bowl, combine the remaining 1 teaspoon salt, cake flour, nutmeg and potato starch and mix well. Sprinkle this mixture and remaining nettle leaves over the even layer of riced potatoes. Using your hands or a spatula, gently fold the dough in on itself to combine the potatoes and flours. Gently flatten out the dough again and taste it for seasoning and adjust as necessary. Then fold in the beaten egg until just combined—do not overmix.

Take about 1½ tablespoons (45 g), about the size of a golf ball, of the dough and gently roll a ball. With your thumb, make a deep impression in the center of each ball and stick a toasted bread cube inside. Close up the dough around the bread cube and gently reshape the dough into a ball and place it on a medium lined baking sheet. Repeat this process with the rest of the dough and bread cubes. The recipe will make about 16 balls.

Add the reserved mushroom water to a large stockpot and add more water until there are about 8 cups (1.9 L) in the pot. Bring the water to a gentle rolling boil over medium-high heat and lightly salt the water. Add the balls in batches of 4 and cook for 12 to 14 minutes. Remove them from the water, let them cool a bit and then toss them in the warm nettle butter and serve with the mushroom and herb mixture. This is an excellent stand-alone dish or goes well with some thinly sliced meats or cold cuts.

Chilled Lemon Nettle Panna Cotta

Savory Panna Cotta with Lemon and Nettles

Serves: 4 — Difficulty level: Easy

This is an elegant little starter dish or substitute for a salad. It's perfect warm-weather food and can be made a day or two in advance. I don't treat this as a "pudding" but rather as something through which to drag small, crunchy crudités. This recipe balances the traditional creaminess of panna cotta with a fresh green flavor and the tartness of lemons. You can either use one large mold that holds 3 cups (720 ml) and serve the panna cotta family-style, or you can use 4 smaller molds that hold ¾ cup (180 ml) each.

2 cups (30 g) densely packed nettle leaves, washed and stemmed

2 tsp (9 g) powdered gelatin

1 cup (240 ml) whole milk, divided

1½ cups (360 ml) heavy cream

1 clove garlic, smashed

1 dried bay leaf

½ tsp sea salt

Freshly ground black pepper to, taste

1 tbsp (15 ml) fresh lemon juice

Zest of 1 lemon

In a medium pot over medium-high heat, bring lightly salted water to a boil and blanch the nettles for 2 minutes. You just want to remove the sting and soften them slightly so you can process them easily and smoothly in the food processor.

Drain the nettles and when they are cool, place them in a clean kitchen towel and gently wring. Set aside. It's OK to have a little moisture left. You'll end up with ¼ cup (4 g) cooked nettles.

Meanwhile, bloom your gelatin and ¼ cup (60 ml) of the milk in a small bowl until the gelatin dissolves. Let the gelatin sit for 5 minutes, stirring a few times to release any clumps from the bottom of the bowl.

In a small pot over medium-high heat, combine the remaining ¾ cup (180 ml) milk, cream, garlic, bay leaf and salt and let the mixture warm until it just simmers (don't let it boil). Gently simmer for 5 minutes and then add the gelatin mixture. Whisk vigorously to break up the gelatin and combine the flavors for another 2 minutes. Turn off the heat and let this mixture cool. Taste to see if you need to adjust the salt or pepper.

When the milk mixture cooled a bit, remove and discard the garlic clove and bay leaf and any larger particles that didn't break down with whisking. Add the mixture to a high-speed processor (or use an immersion blender) along with the lemon juice, lemon zest and blanched nettles. Blend until very smooth, about 3 to 4 minutes, but don't whip the cream.

Strain the mixture, pour into molds and chill in the refrigerator for at least 4 hours. You'll want to cover the molds with plastic wrap to prevent the panna cotta from drying out and prevent a skin from forming. Some of the nettle "sediment" will settle, but it makes for a beautiful green ring pattern.

Turn the panna cotta out onto plates. You may want to dip the bottom of the molds in a shallow pan of warm water to loosen them (and then separate the edges with a sharp paring knife as well) before tipping them onto the plates.

Serve with crudités and crunchy salt and maybe even some homemade crackers.

Nettle Chimichurri and Chipas

Nettle and Herb Sauce with Tapioca Puffs

Serves: 4–6 — Difficulty level: Easy

Chimichurri seems to pop up in many countries in the form of *salsa verde, pistou, sauce verte, Grüne Soße* and many more. More often than not, each country will claim theirs is the best—but even though half of my family is from Argentina, I'll just say that I like them all to be diplomatic.

It seems like many countries have a version of *chipas*: Argentina, Paraguay, Brazil, Colombia, Ecuador, France and many more, I'm sure. Also, sometimes they're called *pan de queso, pan de yuca, pão de queijo* and *gougères*. Chipas, airy cheese puffs made with manioc or tapioca flour, are something your Argentine grandma would let you do slightly unsupervised (minus the hot oil/milk part), because they are really easy to make and very hard to mess up. Rolling the balls keeps little hands busy. The fun is seeing if you can eat them straight out of the oven without steaming your tongue off. When hot, they are crisp on the outside and steamy, soft and chewy on the inside. They get soft as they cool (remember to store them in an airtight container once they are completely cooled) but are easy to crisp back up in the toaster oven for 3 to 4 minutes.

NETTLE CHIMICHURRI

4 cups (60 g) densely packed nettles

2 tbsp (10 g) finely chopped fresh parsley

1 clove garlic, minced

⅛ tsp coarsely ground dried bay leaf

1 tbsp (5 g) finely chopped fresh oregano

⅛ tsp red pepper flakes

¼ cup (60 ml) olive oil

1 tbsp (15 ml) rice vinegar

Sea salt, to taste

NETTLE CHIMICHURRI

In a medium stockpot over high heat, blanch the nettles in moderately salted water for 2 to 3 minutes. You want to cook them just long enough to remove the "sting." Drain the nettles, let them cool and then gently wring the water out by placing them in a clean kitchen towel and very gently squeezing the remainder of the water out. Chop the nettles finely and set aside.

In a medium bowl, combine the nettles, parsley, garlic, bay leaf, oregano, red pepper flakes, olive oil, vinegar and salt and let the chimichurri refrigerate overnight. This recipe makes about 1 cup (240 ml) to 1¼ cups (300 ml). If you'd like a thinner chimichurri, add more oil and vinegar. Use this chimichurri as a pesto, use it as a spread for sandwiches, toss your veggies in it, slather it on toast or drizzle it over eggs or grilled meats. It's pretty much good with anything.

(continued)

CHIPAS

½ cup (120 ml) coconut milk or cow's milk

¼ cup (60 ml) olive oil

1 cup (113 g) tapioca flour or manioc flour

¼ cup (25 g) shredded Parmigiano-Reggiano or Parmesan

½ cup (50 g) shredded Queso Holandita (or any type of Edam cheese)

1 large egg, beaten

Sea salt, to taste

CHIPAS

Preheat the oven to 450°F (232°C) if you will be baking the chipas the same day you make them.

Combine the coconut milk and oil in a small saucepan over medium heat. Whisk the mixture and bring it to a simmer. Take the saucepan off the heat. Let the coconut milk mixture cool for 5 to 7 minutes. While it's still quite warm, whisk in the tapioca flour off the heat until the mixture forms a thick paste. Let this mixture cool completely. Transfer the cooled tapioca mixture to a food processor and process for 2 to 3 minutes. Then add the Parmigiano-Reggiano and Queso Holandita and process for 1 more minute, then add the egg and process until the mixture forms a dough ball. If it's still crumbly and not a smooth dough, add a few drops of hot water while processing until a smooth, shiny, sticky dough forms.

Remove the dough from the processor. On a large baking sheet lined with parchment paper, roll about 20 balls of dough a little smaller than a golf ball (1 to 1½ inches (2.5 to 3 cm), oiling your hands slightly between rolling each chipa. Place the chipas at least 1 inch (3 cm) apart, as they will expand while baking. Cover the baking sheet with oiled plastic wrap and let the chipas chill in the refrigerator for at least 20 minutes or up to overnight. Let the baking sheet sit out at room temperature for 10 minutes before baking if you let the chipas chill overnight. Preheat the oven to 450°F (232°C) while the chipas are warming up.

Place the baking sheet of chipas on the oven's middle rack. Turn down the heat immediately to 350°F (177°C) and bake the chipas for 12 to 15 minutes. Don't open the oven. These are going to take longer than you would think. After 12 minutes, check on them. They should be a little golden on the top and bottom and you should be able to see little browned-cheese specks. They are not going to get super brown, as tapioca flour doesn't darken too much. If after 12 minutes the chipas are not browned even slightly, continue baking for up to 5 to 7 minutes. Note: You can use an egg wash, but a very light one. If you do use an egg wash, dilute it a little with cream or milk and when brushing, try not to let it drop on the pan. Just brush the tops lightly. The high temperature of the oven can burn the egg.

Remove the chipas from the oven and let them cool slightly on a wire rack and then be prepared for the stampede. It's OK if you pop a few in your mouth when no one is looking. Enjoy with some yerba matè, white fir tea and the chimichurri.

Note: This chimichurri recipe can be adapted to any edible wild greens. Nettles just happen to be my favorite and really do lend the most flavor.

Nettles Benedict

Sweet Potato Nests, Poached Quail Eggs and Nettle Hollandaise Sauce

Serves: 4-6 — Difficulty: Moderate

This is a very quick breakfast or brunch idea perfect for entertaining. The hollandaise sauce can be made in less than five minutes in a blender and quail eggs take only a minute to poach. You can omit the sweet potato nests and serve with toast points, as well.

SWEET POTATO NESTS

2 medium sweet potatoes, peeled

2 cups (480 ml) grapeseed oil, for frying

Nettle leaves, washed, thoroughly dried and stemmed, as needed for garnish

QUAIL EGGS

2 tbsp (30 ml) distilled white vinegar

10 quail eggs

SWEET POTATO NESTS

Use a spiral vegetable slicer or, even easier, a julienne peeler to slice the sweet potatoes into ribbons. Soak the ribbons in icy cold water for at least 1 hour. This leaches out some of the starch so the potatoes fry up more crisply. Drain the sweet potato ribbons and pat very dry.

Heat the oil in a small cast iron pan over medium-high heat (the oil should be 1 inch [3 cm] deep). Test it after 3 to 4 minutes with a wooden toothpick or skewer. If the wood "fries," then the oil is up to temperature. If you have a cooking thermometer, the temperature should be 355°F (179°C).

Spray the inside of a 2- or 3-inch (5- or 8-cm) metal cooking or pastry ring with nonstick spray and pack the sweet potato ribbons into the ring as tightly as you can. With a heat-proof spatula or metal fish spatula, gently transfer the packed ring to the hot oil. Let it fry for 1 to 2 minutes and then, with tongs, flip the ring and let it fry for 10 seconds. Using the tongs to hold the ring, push the sweet potato nest out of the ring and into the oil with the back of a spoon and let the exposed sides fry and cook until the sweet potato nest is crisp on all sides. Drain the nest on kitchen paper and salt to taste immediately. Repeat this process with any remaining sweet potato ribbons.

After all the sweet potato nests have been fried, carefully drop the nettle leaves into the oil and fry for 5 to 6 seconds. Drain the nettle leaves on kitchen paper until you are ready to serve.

QUAIL EGGS

Bring a medium stockpot of water to a gentle boil over medium heat and add the vinegar. Submerge a ladle or a slotted spoon in the water and "crack" the quail egg into the submerged ladle or spoon. Move the ladle or spoon around gently while containing the egg for a little less than 1 minute. Transfer the egg to a large bowl of lukewarm water until you are ready to serve. If they get cold, you can quickly flash them in hot water again and drain them on kitchen towels.

(continued)

NETTLE HOLLANDAISE SAUCE

2 cups (30 g) densely packed nettle leaves, washed and stemmed

8 tbsp (112 g) butter

3 large egg yolks

¼ tsp Dijon mustard

Pinch sea salt

Pinch white pepper

1 tbsp (15 ml) fresh lemon juice

NETTLE HOLLANDAISE SAUCE

In a medium stockpot over high heat, blanch the nettles in lightly salted boiling water for 3 to 4 minutes. Drain the nettle leaves, gently wring them dry with a clean kitchen towel and let them cool. Finely chop the nettle leaves and set aside.

In a small saucepan over medium heat, melt the butter until it's a little foamy, skimming off any milk solids from the top. To a blender add the egg yolks, mustard, salt, pepper and lemon juice and blend for 30 seconds until smooth and combined. Add the nettle leaves and blend for 1 to 2 minutes until smooth and combined. While the blender is running, slowly add the butter in a slow and steady stream. It should thicken almost immediately. Taste it and adjust the salt level. Keep the hollandaise sauce warm until serving by transferring it to a heat-proof container (like a mason jar) and place the jar in a small pot of warm water.

Nettle Tamagoyaki

Nettle Omelets with Black Rice

Serves: 4 — Difficulty level: Advanced

Tamagoyaki is a flavorful, thin egg "crêpe" rolled on itself and then sliced and served over rice with some nori and garnishes. It requires a special pan, but since I don't own one, I have made this in a regular round nonstick pan as well as a square nonstick bread pan placed directly on the burner. However, you can make this much easier on yourself by just making a beautiful scramble over rice, or you can use rectangular silicone baking molds and gently steam them for 3 to 4 minutes in a bamboo steamer over a pot of boiling water. However you approach this tamagoyaki, it's a delicious and satisfying egg dish.

1 cup (200 g) black forbidden rice

6 cups (1.4 L) water, divided

1 tsp plus pinch sea salt, divided

3 tbsp (36 g) sugar, divided

1 tbsp (15 ml) rice vinegar

2 cups (30 g) densely packed nettle leaves, washed and stemmed

4 large eggs

1 tsp mirin

1 tsp tamari

½ medium shallot, minced

½ tsp olive oil

2 (7 x 8-inch [18 x 20-cm]) sheets nori

6 tbsp (96 g) salmon roe

Prepare the rice by rinsing it twice in cold water. Drain well and add the rice, 2 cups (480 ml) of the water and the pinch salt to a small stockpot that has a tight-fitting lid. Bring this to a boil over high heat and cook for 45 to 50 minutes. While the rice is cooking, dissolve 2 tablespoons (24 g) of the sugar and ½ teaspoon of the salt in the rice vinegar in a small measuring cup and set aside. Let the cooked rice cool slightly, but while it is still warm sprinkle the vinegar mixture over the rice and gently fold to combine thoroughly. Set aside and let the rice cool. Once cool, make the rice bases for your tamagoyaki by forming a 2-inch (6-cm) ball, pressing it firmly between your hands and shaping it into a tapered oval shape—or you can use a 2-inch (6-cm) cookie cutter or mold, as I did. You should be able to make 8 rice bases with a little extra or 4 bowls of rice if you are topping it with a scramble.

In a medium stockpot over high heat, bring the remaining 4 cups (960 ml) water and the remaining ½ teaspoon salt to a boil. Blanch the nettle leaves for 3 to 4 minutes. This will soften the nettle leaves enough to blend and also make a quick nettle broth that we'll use instead of a traditional dashi. Drain the nettle leaves and reserve ⅛ cup (30 ml) of the nettle broth. Let the nettles and reserved nettle broth cool down.

To a blender or food processor, add the eggs, mirin, tamari, the remaining 1 tablespoon (12 g) sugar, the reserved nettle broth and the shallot and process until smooth and well combined. Let this settle for 10 minutes to release any air bubbles.

Depending on the method you are using, add the oil to a medium nonstick pan and scramble the egg mixture over medium-low heat; roll the egg mixture over medium-low heat; or lightly oil the molds you are using and steam them per the instructions in the recipe headnote. If you are rolling the mixture, you want to pour the egg mixture into the pan until the bottom has set but the top is still a little runny. With a spatula, wedge one side off the pan and fold one-fourth of it onto itself and continue to roll the omelet with your spatula. Remove the tamagoyaki from the pan, let it cool for 5 to 7 minutes and slice. You can cut the nori sheets into strips and wrap the rice base and tamagoyaki and serve with salmon roe. You can also just make fine nori slivers (dried seaweed) and sprinkle them over the dish before serving.

Nettle Crêpes with Nettle and Pea Crème Fraîche

Buttermilk, Nettles and Fresh Peas

Serves: 6 — Difficulty Level: Easy

When nettles are popping up, fresh peas are usually in season, as well. They pair well and this dish just screams springtime. Of all my go-to recipes, this is perhaps one of the easiest. Both the crème fraîche and the crêpe batter need to sit for a while, so prepping this the day before will make this all the easier. The crêpes can easily be made gluten-free with a gluten-free flour blend and it works well.

NETTLE AND PEA CRÈME FRAÎCHE

2 tbsp (30 ml) buttermilk

1 cup (240 ml) heavy cream

½ cup (76 g) shelled fresh peas

2 cups (30 g) densely packed nettle leaves, washed and stemmed

1 tbsp (5 g) finely chopped fresh thyme

½ tsp sea salt

NETTLE CRÊPES

2 large eggs

1¼ cups (300 ml) milk

1 cup (125 g) sifted all-purpose flour

2 tbsp (28 g) butter

½ tsp sea salt

NETTLE AND PEA CRÈME FRAÎCHE

In a jar with a tight-fitting lid, combine the buttermilk and cream. Close the jar and give it a good shake. Leave this at room temperature for 8 hours or up to overnight. It should thicken considerably. Stir the mixture once more and store in the refrigerator.

In a small saucepan over high heat, blanch the peas for 2 to 3 minutes or until just tender. Drain the peas, reserving the cooking water, and set them aside in cold water until you are ready to use them.

Bring the reserved water to a boil over high heat, lightly salt it and blanch the nettle leaves for 3 to 4 minutes. Drain the nettle leaves and gently wring them dry in a clean kitchen towel. Chop the nettle leaves finely and reserve half for the crêpes and half for the crème fraîche.

Once the nettle leaves are cool, remove the peas from the cold water and blend them with half the nettles, crème fraîche, thyme and salt in a blender or food processor.

NETTLE CRÊPES

In a food processor, process the eggs, milk and half the reserved nettle leaves until smooth and well combined. Stir in the flour until smooth. Lastly, stir in the butter until thoroughly combined. Transfer the batter to a container with a tight-fitting lid that can hold at least 2 cups (480 ml) and let it sit for at least 2 hours or refrigerate it overnight. The nettles will settle at the bottom, so stir the batter well before pouring.

In a large, greased nonstick sauté pan over medium heat, spoon or pour about 2 tablespoons (30 ml) batter at a time in the center of the pan and swirl it slightly. Let the crêpe cook for about 2 minutes on one side, gently flip it and cook 1 minute on the other side. Repeat this process with the rest of the batter and stack the cooked crêpes inside a clean tea towel until ready to serve or store in an airtight container for future use. I like to serve these with a dollop of the crème fraîche, lox or smoked salmon.

Fragrant Corncake with *Nettles* and Lobster Mushrooms

Nettle and Mushroom Cornbread

Serves: 6-8 — Difficulty level: Easy

I am a fan of cornbread especially if it is not cloyingly sweet. I adore the flavor of fresh summer corn and this dish makes a nice gluten-free alternative when entertaining. It's a wonderful starter dish if served with homemade butter and relish or a great accompaniment to a light soup or salad. Nettles can have an almost seafood-like fragrance and lobster mushrooms have a sea essence as well, along with a meaty texture. These in combination with the sweet pop of fresh corn make the dish. If you don't have access to foraged lobster mushrooms, you can substitute them with any fragrant mushrooms, like dried maitake or porcini.

4 cups (60 g) densely packed nettle leaves, washed and stemmed

3 cups (25 g) dried lobster mushrooms

1 tbsp (15 ml) olive oil

1 medium shallot, finely chopped

1 tsp plus pinch sea salt, divided

1½ cups (250 g) fresh corn kernels

1 tbsp (5 g) finely chopped fresh marjoram

¼ cup plus 2 tbsp (159 g) corn flour

1 cup plus 3 tbsp (190 g) white rice flour

¼ cup (48 g) sugar

8 tbsp (112 g) softened butter

1 tsp baking soda

1 tsp baking powder

¼ tsp xanthan gum

2 large eggs

¾ cup (180 ml) buttermilk

Freshly ground black pepper, to taste

Preheat the oven to 350°F (177°C).

Bring lightly salted water to a boil in a medium stockpot over high heat and blanch the nettle leaves for 3 to 4 minutes. Drain the nettle leaves and when they have cooled, gently wring them dry in a clean kitchen towel, chop finely and reserve. Transfer 3 cups (720 ml) of the hot nettle broth to a medium bowl and rehydrate the mushrooms for at least 1 hour. Strain the mushrooms, chop finely and reserve.

Heat the oil in a medium sauté pan over medium heat. Add the shallot and the pinch salt and cook until the shallot is translucent, 3 to 4 minutes. Add the corn, nettles, mushrooms and marjoram and sauté another 5 to 6 minutes.

In a stand mixer (by hand in a large bowl), combine the corn flour, rice flour, sugar, 1 teaspoon salt and butter until the mixture is uniform and creamy looking, about 5 minutes. Then add the baking soda, baking powder, xanthan gum, eggs, buttermilk and pepper and mix for another 3 to 4 minutes. Fold in the corn mixture.

Line the bottom of a 7-inch (18-cm) spring form pan with a circular piece of parchment paper. Grease the sides of the pan and the parchment. Alternatively, use a greased 8 x 8-inch (20 x 20-cm) cake pan or 9 x 5-inch (23 x 13-cm) loaf pan.

Pour the batter into the prepared pan and bake for 55 to 60 minutes on a sheet tray on the middle oven rack. Start checking the cake at 50 minutes by inserting a sharp knife or toothpick in the center. When the corncake is done, it will come out clean. Let the corncake cool for 10 minutes and then remove it from the pan and put it on a baking rack to cool completely, or enjoy it warm. Wrap any leftovers tightly in a zip-top plastic bag. It's wonderful the next day, sliced and toasted. I like to serve this with clotted cream and honey, too.

Moules et Orties

Mussels and Nettles

Serves: 2-4 — Difficulty level: Easy

My spouse and partner is Belgian, and he loves both mussels and nettles (*moules et orties* in French). I make this dish for him frequently during nettle season. I have always said that I think nettles have a special affinity for eggs and shellfish. Sometimes I'll make a crabmeat and nettle omelet with lots of fresh raw butter, and it has such a roundness, balance and satisfying quality. Beyond delicious. But I digress.

Mussels are one of the easiest things to cook. We have an excellent fishmonger near us, as well as a really knowledgeable sea forager, and we're able to get the freshest seafood available. This recipe will work with frozen mussels but may not have that special texture or brininess that fresh-from-the-sea items offer. If you use frozen mussels, follow the package's thawing and cooking instructions.

2 tbsp (30 ml) olive oil, divided

4 oz (100 g) lardons or roughly chopped bacon, pancetta or other fatty, cured pork

3 medium shallots, minced

½ medium carrot, finely chopped

1 small celery stalk, finely chopped

½ tsp sea salt, plus more to taste

1 clove garlic, finely chopped

2 cups (480 ml) water

½ cup (120 ml) dry sherry or white wine

4 cups (60 g) densely packed nettle leaves, washed and stemmed, divided

5-6 black peppercorns, crushed

1 lb (455 g) fresh mussels (see note)

Heat 1 tablespoon (15 ml) of the oil in a medium saucepan over medium heat. Add the lardons and cook until browned, stirring occasionally, 7 to 10 minutes. Then add the shallots, carrots, celery, the remaining 1 tablespoon (15 ml) oil and salt. Sautè until the celery and onions are just translucent, about 5 to 6 minutes more. Add the garlic and cook another 2 minutes, stirring frequently so as not to burn the garlic. Add the water and sherry, 3½ cups (53 g) nettle leaves and peppercorns and cook, uncovered, another 10 minutes at a gentle simmer or until the liquid reduces slightly. Next, add the mussels and cover the saucepan. Give the pan a good shake to distribute everything. Cook, covered, for 5 more minutes. Taste for salt and adjust if necessary. Discard any mussels that haven't opened.

Roughly chop the remaining ½ cup (7 g) nettle leaves, add them to the saucepan, cover the saucepan and cook for 3 to 4 minutes. Serve the mussels individually or family-style in the middle of the table as a starter dish.

Note: Even if you have an excellent fishmonger, you'll want to give your mussels an extra scrub and be sure to remove any beards or debris from the shells. Discard any mussels that are not tightly closed or have cracks in the shell. Give the remaining mussels a good soak for at least 1 hour in very cold water. If you are not cooking them the minute you get home from the market, store the freshly scrubbed, soaked and drained mussels on ice in an open bag in the fridge. They need to breathe until you cook them.

Ten-Minute Nettle Tonic

Nettle, Ginger and Kelp Broth

Serves: 6–8 — Difficulty level: Easy

Having dried nettles throughout the year is really handy, and dried nettles are even more versatile than fresh sometimes. Also, prepping them is extremely easy. Dehydrating or drying removes the sting, so blanching is not necessary. With scissors and tongs, I separate the leaves and stems from the main stalk and just dehydrate the lot and store them in an airtight container with a tiny bit of kitchen paper towel to keep moisture away. To that end, I am a fan of dehydrating things for future use in general, because they are good pantry staples and keep for a long time.

This ten-minute broth is something I make if I'm feeling a little under the weather, and I don't have the energy to make a complex soup stock from scratch. It's restorative, nutrient-rich, mild, light, calming and quick to make. I add buckwheat noodles for some bulk, but sometimes I make just the broth and carry it around with me in a humongous mason jar and sip at it for a few hours until I'm feeling better. I add whatever foraged ingredients I happen to have—here, I use some cattail shoots and radish flowers.

This broth is intentionally very mild, but if you'd like to add saltiness, I suggest 2 tablespoons (30 ml) tamari, 2 tablespoons (72 g) miso or 2 teaspoons (10 g) good mineral-based salt (such as Himalayan, French *sel gris* or Hawaiian volcanic salt). Keep in mind that you are cooking this uncovered for 10 minutes at a good rolling boil and it will reduce a little, making it saltier. Also, I suggest that this serves 6 to 8 people, but when I make this, it's mainly just for me to sip throughout the day as a tonic.

1 (9.5-oz [270-g]) package buckwheat soba noodles

12 cups (2.9 L) water

1 (2-inch [6-cm]) ginger, peeled and cut into 4 (½-inch [13-mm] thick) rounds

2 cloves garlic, smashed

4 tsp (20 ml) fresh lemon juice

4 cups (12 g) loosely packed dried nettles leaves and stems

1 tbsp (15 ml) liquid aminos, such as Bragg Liquid Aminos

1 cup (10 g) shaved bonito flakes

1 (4–5-inch [10–13-cm]) strip kombu

½ cup (3.5 g) dried, flaked oyster mushrooms

Cook the soba noodles according to the package's instructions. (They are typically boiled for 4 minutes.) Drain the noodles and chill them in a bowl of cold water to stop the cooking process. Set aside.

In a large pot over high heat, add the water, ginger, garlic, lemon juice, nettle leaves and stems, liquid aminos, bonito flakes, kombu and mushrooms and bring to a boil. Reduce the heat to medium-low and cook for 10 minutes. Turn off the heat and let the mixture "steep" for at least 20 minutes. It should be cool enough to eat by then. Remove and discard the kombu, garlic and ginger. Add as many cooked soba noodles as you'd like and serve.

Nettle Bagna Cauda

Nettle and Anchovy Sauce

Serves: 4-6 — Difficulty level: Easy

I'll admit I have a penchant for small, oily fishes like anchovies, smelt, herring and sprats. They are a good pantry staple to have on hand, add incredible flavor to almost anything, are sustainable and are also a great source of omega-3s. Anchovies are a favorite of mine—fresh, dried, jarred or canned. I'll use them in place of salt in a simple tossed pasta dish or as a spread on bread. If you're thinking anchovies are fishy or too strong, you might have to change your mind for this very basic but classic recipe. Even kids get addicted to this. The secret is low-and-slow cooking.

This is another dish where I am using nettles as an herb. All the ingredients melt together and become indistinguishable from the rest, creating an entirely new flavor. The garlic and anchovies mellow considerably and the cooking method really pulls the nettle flavor out. Plus, this is an indispensable way to feature other foraged goodies like cattail, rattail radishes, thistle stems, wild lettuces or any of your garden or yard goodies. This sauce freezes well, but I doubt you'll have any left.

3 cups (45 g) densely packed nettle leaves, washed and stemmed

½ cup (115 g) butter

½ cup (120 ml) olive oil

8–10 anchovy fillets (¼ cup [40g]) in olive oil (see note)

½ cup (120 ml) Spanish sherry

5 cloves garlic, smashed

Pinch sea salt

Pinch red pepper flakes, optional

Preheat the oven to 225°F (107°C).

In a medium stockpot over high heat, blanch the nettles in lightly salted boiling water for 2 to 3 minutes. Drain the nettle leaves and gently wring them dry using a clean kitchen towel. Chop finely and reserve.

In a small, oven-safe, heavy-bottomed pot over low heat, melt the butter with the oil. Add the anchovy fillets, sherry, garlic, salt and red pepper flakes and bring to just a simmer and then turn off the heat. Make sure all the ingredients are submerged under the melted butter and oil by ½ inch (13 mm).

Place the pot on a baking sheet and bake, uncovered, for about 3 hours. Add the finely chopped nettles to the pot during the last hour of cooking. The solid ingredients should have disintegrated and the bagna cauda should have a toasty, nutty, mellow flavor. Serve warm in the center of the table, family-style, with cool veggies or on just about anything else you have. If you freeze this, you can make an excellent side dish in a few minutes by tossing boiled new potatoes in the reheated sauce.

Note: I really like Spanish anchovies packed in olive oil, but you can use any preserved or dried anchovies. You'll need to add a bit of salt to fresh anchovies, but they will work, too. If you use the dried ones packed in salt, give them several good rinses with cold water or they will be too salty.

Nettle-Ade

Nettles, Honey and Preserved Lemon

Serves: 8 — Difficulty level: Easy

In addition to broths, dried nettles are a staple for teas in my house. Nettles are nutrient-rich, and they also help me manage springtime allergies. I'm not a medical professional, but traditional and homeopathic medicine supports this as well. This drink is simple to make, a little unusual and delicious.
I borrowed inspiration from Vietnamese *chanh muối* (preserved lime) soda.

Dried nettle leaves and stems, as needed (see note)

Boiling water, as needed (see note)

Ice, as needed

1 tbsp (15 ml) honey per serving

⅛ preserved lemon (or a ½-inch [1.5-cm] chunk) per serving

1 cup (240 ml) sparkling water per serving

To steep the dried nettles, place the nettles in a teapot or a nonreactive pot and pour the boiling water over them. Let the nettles steep for 15 minutes, then strain them from the water.

Add ice to a tall glass and muddle the honey with the preserved lemon. Pour in ½ cup (120 ml) of the strong nettle tea and finish with the sparkling water.

Note: A general rule of thumb is to use 1 tablespoon (1 g) dried nettles per 1 cup (240 ml) water. But I like to make this strong so I can enjoy it with ice and sparkling water, so I use 2 tablespoons (2 g) dried nettles per 1 cup (240 ml) water. For example, to make 4 servings, use 8 teaspoons (6 g) nettles and 4 cups (960 ml) water. It's OK to eyeball this, as dried nettles weigh practically nothing and you won't get a significant measurement by weight.

Chapter Six

Dandelions and Curly Dock

Two Flavors in One

Oh, hardy flower, disdained as weed, despised for head of feathery seed,
your unsung virtues rate a ballad, choice roots for wine, crisp leaves for salad.

– Betty Gay

Dandelions and curly dock are interesting plants to me because they urge you to pull out some creativity. These are also two plants that many people forage, but they can seem like one-trick ponies. Even in vintage cookbooks, I have trouble finding more than a handful of recipes for each, yet both are praised in older books for heralding spring and cleansing the body. It seems like these two plants have receded into the past as far as use and recipes go, but they are both extremely abundant, and I think they deserve a more prominent place in modern cooking.

I think once you understand the flavor profiles of both, you can see where you can incorporate them or substitute them in your dishes. Both plants have dual characteristics that need a little taming. For example, both have a bitter, tannic quality that can seem unappealing but both also have subtle, complementary flavors—dandelions are a little meaty yet sweet and herbal, and curly dock has a gentle lemony yet verdant flavor.

Flowering dandelion (*Taraxacum officinale*)

Dandelion

Taraxacum officinale

Asteraceae family, Cichorioideae (chicory) subfamily

Native and introduced to North America; invasive

Flavor Profile

As a member of the chicory family, dandelion shares that bitter aftertaste, but when the leaves are relatively young, you can coax a sweetness out of them. The texture of dandelion depends on the age and size of the plant, but various cooking and prepping methods can change both the flavor and texture. I like the bitterness when combined with some foods. It's all about balance. The entire plant can be utilized, whether as food or medicine.

When and How to Harvest

From winter to early summer, in my area, you can harvest the young flowers before they form a "choke" and sauté them or fry them. Many people make dandelion tea, jelly and wine. The roots have medicinal uses, but I mainly use the leaves. I harvest the plant by taking one-third or half of the plant. Often, someone will call me to remove the entire plant from their garden. Dandelion, believed to one of the oldest of plants, is also one of the hardiest. They can grow in hard, compacted poor soils as well as fertile, well-drained soils. Just look at where you see them: in fields, in yards, sometimes in the middle of a dry field alone and sometimes near a water spigot. These are easy to spot, especially with their distinct yellow flower and soft white puff when they go to seed. There are a few look-alikes, however, which I'll mention shortly.

Distinguishing Identifiers

- Rosette growth pattern—Long leaves with runcinated pattern (they look like a series of arrows, pointing backward)

- Buttercup yellow floret and fluffy seeds (although several other plants have this, too)

Possible Look-Alikes

- Sow-thistle
- False dandelion
- Groundsel
- Cat's ear
- Desert chicory
- Mountain dandelion

Curly Dock

Rumex crispus

Polygonaceae family

Native and introduced to
North America; invasive

Curly Dock (*Rumex crispus*)

Flavor Profile

Depending on the time of the season and the location in which you harvest, curly dock's flavor can be lemony and light, sour and astringent or tart and bitter. You can control the tannic taste a bit with blanching, but the plant is best in early spring.

Curly dock growing in a semi-sunny location with little water and poor sandy soil has a tendency to be quite tart and bitter and tough.

Note: This plant contains a high amount of oxalic acid, known to cause kidney stones in some people, and should be eaten in moderation.

When and How To Harvest

I have seen this plant come to life year-round if there's any moisture in the soil at all. When the temperature outside gets really hot, curly dock is often the last thing standing. It is definitely a plant you want to forage in shady and humid locations, preferably in or near a stream. Watch for pollution if you pick it up from water, and don't forget the rule to harvest it 1 to 2 inches (3 to 6 cm) above the water level. I harvest the younger shoots and leaves when juicing or preparing raw dishes, and I use the larger leaves for cooking.

Distinguishing Identifiers

- Basal rosette pattern
- Long, smooth, tender leaves that are slightly "corrugated" or jagged
- Small flowers with triangular seeds that turn a bright rust color

Possible Look-Alikes

- Primrose
- Perennial pepperweed

Creamed Dandelion

Creamed Dandelion with Mace, Pearl Onions and Bacon

Serves 4–6 — Difficulty level: Easy

If you have someone in your life who doesn't eat dandelions, this is a nice gateway dish. I love the bitterness of the plant because it acts like a contrast to the other flavors. This is an interesting side dish and is great for entertaining. It's comforting and a little elegant at the same time. The sweetness of the chicory powder balances the cream and dandelions. Just remember to wash your dandelion greens well by soaking them. If you are collecting them from a field or your yard, it seems like a few strands of grass always sneak in. Cut or trim any damaged or really tough ends. It can get a little chewy and tough closer to the root.

10–12 large pearl onions

4 (1-inch [3-cm] thick) strips bacon

4 cups (220 g) dandelion greens, washed, trimmed and roughly chopped

2 cloves garlic, minced

3 cups (720 ml) heavy cream

¼ tsp plus pinch sea salt

½ tsp ground mace

1 tsp chicory powder

Cut the root ends off the pearl onions and boil them in a medium pot over high heat for 3 to 4 minutes. Drain the onions and let them cool enough to handle. Squeeze the onions to pop out the centers. (If they are still giving you a little trouble, cut off the other end of the onions and squeeze them out. Be careful, though—if you do it that way, they tend to shoot across the room.) Cut the onions in half and set aside.

Cut the bacon into thin lardons. Dry the pot that was used to cook the onions and return it to medium-high heat. Add the lardons and brown until crisp, about 5 to 7 minutes. Add the dandelion greens and garlic and cook for 1 more minute, tossing to coat them in the bacon fat. Pour in the cream and add the pearl onions, salt, mace and chicory powder.

Bring the mixture to a boil over medium-high heat, being careful not to scald the cream, then reduce the heat to medium-low and bring the mixture to barely a simmer. Cook, uncovered, for 40 minutes, stirring occasionally. Taste for salt and adjust as needed.

I usually serve this with little chicory-crusted game hens. They cook in about the same time as the dandelion greens.

Note: Chicory powder is made from chicory, which is related to the dandelion plant. The roots are made into a coffee substitute and it's often sold already sweetened as an instant "coffee." Unsweetened chicory is also available, however. If you are using that, mix it with a little sugar using the ratio of two parts chicory powder to one part sugar.

Dandy Salad

Dandelion Greens, Blueberries, Kiwi and Green Tea-Mint Salt

Serves: 4 — Difficulty level: Easy

This is yet another recipe that the dandelion averse may try. The leaves do retain their bitterness, but the fruit balances with sweetness and the fat of the avocados cuts the sharpness.
It's a super clean and healthful salad—not to mention beautiful!

2 tbsp (4 g) dried mint

2 tbsp (11 g) matcha tea

1 tbsp (15 g) coarse sea salt

8 cups (440 g) washed, trimmed and roughly chopped dandelion

Juice and zest of 2 limes

2 tbsp (30 ml) olive oil

2 cups (298 g) blueberries, washed and dried

2 medium kiwis, peeled and thinly sliced

1 small bunch fresh mint, washed and stemmed

2 medium avocados, peeled, pitted and thinly sliced

To make the green tea-mint salt, add the dried mint, matcha powder and coarse salt to a clean espresso grinder. Process into a medium-fine powder and store in an airtight container.

In a large bowl, add the dandelion, lime juice, zest and the oil. Toss to combine and coat everything. Let this mixture marinate for 10 minutes. Add the blueberries, kiwis and fresh mint and gently toss. Layer the avocados on top, sprinkle with green tea salt to taste and serve.

The Bittersweet Onion

Dandelion Greens, Walnut and Date Stuffed Sweet Onions with Cognac

Serves: 2 — Difficulty level: Easy

This is an wonderful dish that takes advantage of common things you may have in your pantry, especially during the holiday season. This dish balances sweet, bitter, rich and savory all with relatively humble ingredients as common as an onion. It's an excellent elegant starter.

2 large white or sweet onions

3 cups (165 g) dandelion greens, washed, trimmed and finely chopped

1 tbsp (15 ml) olive oil

3 tbsp (42 g) butter, cubed, divided

½ tsp plus pinch sea salt, divided

½ tsp dried marjoram

½ medium celery stalk, minced

½ medium carrot, finely chopped

1 clove garlic, minced

2 tbsp (15 g) toasted and roughly chopped walnuts

2 large or 4 small dried dates, pitted and finely chopped

1 cup (35 g) 1-inch (3-cm) sourdough bread cubes

2 tbsp (30 ml) cognac or brandy

Preheat the oven to 425°F (218°C).

Cut the top thirds of the onions off. Make a small cut to the root ends without removing the roots, so that the onions will stay upright during baking. Using a paring knife, cut the centers out of each onion. With a spoon (a grapefruit spoon works well if you have one), scoop out the centers of the onions and reserve 2 tablespoons (20 g) of the middle of the onions. You want to leave the two outermost thick layers intact, so that the onion keeps its structure during baking.

In a shallow oven-safe dish, place the onions, root ends down, and fill the dish with about 1 inch (3 cm) of water. Cover the dish with aluminum foil and bake for 35 to 40 minutes. The onions should soften and be slightly translucent on the edges.

While the onions are precooking in the oven, chop 2 tablespoons (20 g) of the onion cores and set aside. You can freeze the rest for future use.

In a small pot over high heat, blanch the dandelion greens in lightly salted boiling water for 3 to 4 minutes. Drain the dandelion greens, pat them dry, roughly chop and set aside.

Heat the oil and 1 tablespoon (14 g) of the butter in a medium sauté pan over medium heat. Add the chopped onion, salt, marjoram, celery and carrot and cook for 5 to 6 minutes or until soft. Add the garlic and cook for 1 more minute. Add the dandelions, walnuts, dates and bread cubes and toss until well coated and combined.

Divide 1 tablespoon (14 g) of butter between the bottoms of the onions. Top the butter with a pinch salt, stuff the onion as tightly as you can with the vegetable stuffing, pour 1 tablespoon (15 ml) cognac over the top of each onion and top with the rest of the butter.

Bring the oven temperature down to 375°F (191°C) and bake the onions uncovered for another 40 minutes. If you like the skin crispy, you can butter the outsides of the onions and use a small kitchen torch before serving. Let the onions cool a bit before serving.

Salted Dandelion and Plantain Two Ways

Serves 2 — Difficulty level: Easy

At times, wild food (especially greens) can be a little bitter and sometimes tough, depending on the weather conditions and amount of water they have received. For many foragers, the most satisfying thing is to be able to adapt and use what you have. I think this preparation method lets dandelions sing. The technique is nothing new. Many Asian, Mediterranean and other cultures prepare greens in a similar way. I find this is versatile for dandelion greens and broad leaf plantain. It breaks them down enough to avoid toughness, enables them to absorb flavors, gets rid of a bit of the bitterness, and still retains a wonderful texture.

6 cups (330 g) densely packed dandelion leaves, washed

2 cups (40 g) densely packed broad leaf plantain leaves, washed

1 heaping tbsp (18 g) sea salt

1 tbsp (15 ml) vegetable oil

2 cloves garlic, thinly sliced

¼ tsp tamari

¼ tsp sesame oil

2 tbsp (30 ml) seasoned rice vinegar

1 tbsp (15 g) pickled minced ginger

2 tbsp (20 g) roughly chopped fresh cilantro

1 cup (176 g) cooked rice noodles

½ medium jalapeño, thinly sliced

Trim off parts of the dandelion stems and plantain stems that will be too chewy or tough. If the plantain leaves are large, cut them into manageable strips. In a medium bowl, gently massage the leaves with the salt until they shrink and turn darker green in color, 2 to 3 minutes. Let them sit at room temperature for about 15 to 20 minutes. Don't crush the leaves and stems while you massage them—the salt, wilting time and blanching will soften them sufficiently.

Rinse the leaves well in cold water. In a medium pot over medium-high heat, bring water to a boil and blanch the greens for 3 to 4 minutes to remove the salt. Shock them in cold water to stop the cooking process and then very gently pat them dry with a clean kitchen towel. Set aside.

Heat the vegetable oil in a small sautè pan over medium heat. Add the garlic and cook for 2 to 3 minutes or until light golden brown. Remove the garlic from the pan and let cool. In a large bowl, combine the tamari, sesame oil, vinegar, ginger and cilantro and mix well. Fold in the noodles and greens, mixing to coat. Check for seasoning and add salt and pepper to taste. Top with jalapeño slices. I personally love to make very minimalist dishes with these leaves. My favorite way to eat them is cold, dressed with the tamari, vinegar and oil and topped with the jalapeño.

Here are some other flavor combinations I love with salted dandelion and plantain:

Lemon, olive oil, garlic, fresh oregano

Tahini, harissa vinaigrette, fried eggplant chunks

Tamari, chili, cilantro, sesame oil, ginger

Rosemary, olive oil, white fir vinegar, garlic confit, white beans

Days of *figs* and Wine

Braised Dandelion Greens with Caramelized Figs and Onions in Red Wine

Serves: 2-4 — Difficulty level: Easy

This dish was inspired by a leftover half bottle of wine and a plethora of dandelions in my yard. In addition, my dear friend gifted me the most amazing figs from her trees. All these ingredients made me think of the goat Gouda I had in the fridge, and then my mouth really started to water. This is an excellent side dish to game meat, red meat or pork.

2 tbsp (28 g) butter, divided

1 tbsp (15 ml) olive oil

1 medium onion, halved and cut into ⅛-inch (3-mm) thick half-moons

1 tsp finely chopped fresh rosemary

4 cloves garlic, minced

½ tsp plus pinch sea salt, divided

1 tbsp (15 ml) good-quality balsamic vinegar

2 cups (480 ml) vegetable or chicken stock

½ cup (120 ml) dry red wine

Pinch sugar

8 cups (440 g) dandelion leaves, washed, trimmed and roughly chopped

4 large fresh figs

1 (2-oz [57-g]) piece aged goat Gouda or Spanish Manchego, frozen

Heat 1 tablespoon (14 g) of the butter and the oil in a medium, heavy-bottomed stockpot over low heat. Add the onion. Cook, stirring occasionally, until the onion is caramelized, 35 to 40 minutes. Add the rosemary, garlic and a pinch of salt during the last 5 minutes of cooking.

Deglaze the pot with the balsamic vinegar, scraping any bits from the bottom with a wooden spoon. Add the stock, wine, sugar and the remaining ½ teaspoon salt. Bring the pot up to a boil and then lower the heat to medium-low and bring to a simmer. Add the dandelion leaves, braise them for 45 minutes partially covered. Taste for salt and sugar and adjust accordingly.

Wash the figs and trim the tops and bottoms. Slice the figs into ¼-inch (6-mm) thick rings. To a small sauté pan over medium-high heat, add the remaining 1 tablespoon (14 g) butter and brown one side of the figs for 2 to 3 minutes. Remove the figs from the heat and set aside.

To serve, arrange the dandelion leaves in a large bowl or deep platter. Scatter the figs over the top and, with a rasp grater, grate the frozen cheese lightly over the top.

Russian *Curly* Pockets

Curly Dock, Sprats and Groats in a Caraway Pita

Serves 4–6 — Difficulty level: Easy

This is a satisfying salad filled with flavorful surprises, but the backbone is definitely the ribbons of slightly tart and tannic curly dock greens. It's similar to a crunch salad I make and has so many different textures as well as a little touch of horseradish and caraway from the pita. It's also a balanced meal with protein, whole grains and greens. One of my good friends says it reminds her of a fancy tuna fish sandwich. I like that.

I used sprats in this dish, which are small, sustainable little forage fish eaten all around the world and are popular in Europe. They usually come in a 9.5-ounce (270-g) jar packed in olive oil and are smoked for added flavor. They also come in 5.6-ounce (160-g) tins. Note: You can use tuna fish in this recipe, but if you do, try the tuna packed in olive oil. It's more flavorful and moist. You can also use herring, kippers, sardines or any other little oily fish.

You can eat the salad as is in a bowl or in lettuce cups, but I like to serve this with homemade Caraway Pitas (page 139).

½ cup (85 g) buckwheat groats

1 cup (240 ml) plus 1 tsp water

1 clove garlic, smashed

1 dried bay leaf

2 pinches sea salt, divided

4 cups (120 g) curly dock leaves, washed and stemmed

1 tbsp (15 ml) olive oil

1 tbsp (15 ml) apple cider vinegar

1 tsp finely grated fresh horseradish

Freshly ground black pepper, to taste

6 oz (170 g) sprats

3 tbsp (15 g) minced fresh tarragon

1 tbsp (5 g) minced fresh parsley

1 medium celery stalk, finely chopped

½ small red onion, finely chopped

½ cup (50 g) fresh snap peas, roughly chopped

3 tbsp (25 g) capers, roughly chopped

Toast the buckwheat groats in a medium, heavy-bottomed or cast iron pan until fragrant and browned by swirling them around a dry pan over medium-high heat for 3 to 4 minutes. Remove the groats from the pan immediately and set aside.

In a small pot over medium-high heat, bring the water to a boil. Add the groats, garlic, bay leaf and 1 pinch of the salt. Cook for 15 to 20 minutes, until the groats are tender. Fluff the groats and set aside.

Stack the curly dock leaves on themselves and then roll them into a tight cylindrical shape. With a very sharp knife, cut the curly dock leaves into fine ribbons crosswise. The curly dock will discolor with a metal knife and it bruises easily, so having a sharp knife and cutting the leaves all at once minimizes these effects. Set the ribbons aside.

Make the salad dressing in a small bowl by whisking together the oil, vinegar, horseradish, the remaining pinch salt and pepper.

In a large bowl, break the sprats apart slightly. Add the groats, curly dock ribbons, tarragon, parsley, celery, onion, snap peas and capers. Mix everything together, drizzle the salad dressing over the salad and toss. Taste for salt and pepper and adjust as needed. Stuff the salad into warm, fresh, homemade pitas.

*See photo on page 124.

Caraway Pitas

Savory Caraway-Spiced Bread

Makes: 12–15 mini pitas — **Difficulty level:** Easy

I can't express how easy pita bread is to make. I like it because it's more compact and versatile than loaf bread and I could just kick myself when I buy it. This simple recipe takes very little effort and the only time involved is rise time.

¾ cup (180 ml) warm water

½ (¼-oz [7-g]) package active dry yeast

1¾ cups (222 g) bread flour

1 tsp black caraway seeds

½ tsp sea salt

½ tsp sugar

1½ tbsp (23 ml) olive oil

Put the warm water in a small bowl, and bloom the yeast by sprinkling it over the water, stirring briefly and letting it sit for 5 to 7 minutes or until it froths.

In a food processor fitted with the dough blade, add the flour, caraway seeds, salt and sugar and pulse to combine. Add the oil to the yeast mixture and drizzle it into the processor slowly while processing on low. The flour mixture should start to form a ball of dough. Knead on low for 5 minutes to develop the gluten. (You can also knead the dough by hand for 5 minutes.)

Remove the dough from the machine, form it into a ball and place it in an oiled medium bowl. Cover the bowl with oiled plastic wrap and let the dough rise for 1½ hours in a warm, non-drafty place.

Preheat the oven to 500°F (260°C). If you have a pizza stone, preheat this as well; otherwise preheat 2 large, heavy baking sheets.

After the dough has doubled in size, punch it down lightly and form 1-ounce (30-g) balls and cover them with a clean, damp kitchen towel. Let them rise again for 10 minutes. On a lightly floured surface, roll the balls out to about ⅛-inch (3-mm) thick. The dough may shrink after you roll it out. Stretch the circles of dough to reshape them a bit before baking. Gently place them directly on the hot pizza stone or baking sheets. Bake for 5 to 6 minutes. With tongs, remove the pitas and let them cool under a dish towel so they don't dry out while they cool. You'll probably have to make these in two or three batches, depending on your equipment. Once the pitas are cool, store them in an airtight container or zip-top bag for up to 5 days. They reheat and crisp up nicely.

Note: The pitas tend to puff up significantly but will deflate as they cool.

Curly Curd Mini Meringues

Curly Dock and Sweet Meringue

Serves: 10 — Difficulty level: Easy

At certain times of the season (early spring in my part of the country), the curly dock is positively lemony and at other times it's more insipid. If I'm lucky enough to happen on the tart version, I'll made a little curd. The flavor is hard to explain. There's definitely a green note, not quite vegetal, and the tartness isn't citrus-like but more akin to tart grapes. It makes for a subtle curd and it goes so well with ripe nectarines.

CURLY DOCK CURD

3 cups (90 g) curly dock leaves, washed and stemmed

8 tbsp (112 g) butter

Pinch sea salt

1 cup (192 g) sugar

4 large egg yolks

MERINGUES

4 large egg whites, at room temperature

1¼ cups (240 g) sugar

⅛ tsp pure vanilla extract

2 tsp (6 g) cornstarch

1 tsp distilled white vinegar

CURLY DOCK CURD

In either an electric or hand-crank juicer, juice the curly dock. You want ½ cup (120 ml) of curly dock liquid. If the curly dock does not provide enough liquid on its own, add a little water to compensate. In a food processor, add the butter, salt and sugar and cream them for 1 minute. Add the egg yolks, one at a time, incorporating them fully before adding another. Lastly, add the curly dock juice and process for 1 minute. It's going to curdle, but it will pull together as it cooks.

Transfer the curly dock mixture to a small stockpot and simmer for 7 to 10 minutes. The mixture should thicken enough to cover the back of a spoon. Transfer the curd to a bowl to cool down and cover the bowl with plastic wrap to prevent a skin forming on the surface of the curd. It should thicken more as it cools.

MERINGUES

Preheat the oven to 250°F (121°C). With a hand blender, beat the egg whites until frothy in a medium bowl. Gradually add the sugar in fourths until you reach stiff but not dry peaks. Add the vanilla with the last of the sugar. Sprinkle the cornstarch over the meringue and sprinkle the vinegar over the cornstarch. Gently fold the mixture thoroughly but do not deflate it. Scoop the meringue into a pastry bag with a 1-inch (3-cm) tip (or you can use a zip-top bag with a corner snipped off). Pipe 1½-inch (4-cm) spirals on a large baking sheet lined with parchment paper. With the back of a wet spoon, make a depression in the middle of each meringue and swoop across and up to form a little cup.

Bake the meringues about 50 minutes and then turn down the heat to 200°F (93°C), crack the oven door open slightly and bake for another 20 minutes. Check the meringues at 20 minutes to see if they are browning too quickly. To serve, spoon about 1 teaspoon of the curly dock curd into each meringue. I top mine with a thin slice of fresh nectarine and some finely chopped mint leaves.

Poisson Cru with Shaved *Curly Dock*

Marinated Raw Fish, Curly Dock and Coconut Milk

Serves: 2 — Difficulty level: Easy

This is definitely not an everyday dish but it's something decadent and tropical and reminds me of my time visiting Tahiti. *Poisson cru* is a very basic dish of fresh, raw fish marinated in lime juice and fresh coconut cream (which is fattier than coconut milk), tomatoes and scallions. There's not a lot to it, just acid, fatty coconut cream, silky fish and fresh vegetables. Because I think dock goes so well with fish and dairy-like fat, this is a match.

4 cups (120 g) curly dock leaves, washed and stemmed, divided

2 tbsp (30 ml) water

¼ tsp plus pinch sea salt, divided

6 oz (170 g) fresh sushi-grade ahi tuna, cut into bite-size cubes

1 cup (240 ml) fresh coconut cream

1 scallion, green and white parts finely chopped

1 medium tomato, cut into ½-inch (13-mm) cubes

1 small Persian cucumber, cut into ¼-inch (6-mm) cubes

Roughly chop 2 cups (60 g) of the curly dock. To a small blender, add the chopped curly dock, water and the pinch salt. Blend well and set aside.

Make fine ribbons with the remaining 2 cups (60 g) curly dock by rolling the leaves into a tight cylindrical shape and cutting crosswise with a sharp knife. Set aside.

In a medium bowl, pour the curly dock marinade over the ahi tuna and gently toss. You'll see the color change a bit as the marinade "cooks" the fish. Let this marinate for 1 minute, and drain the excess liquid from the bowl. Add the remaining ¼ teaspoon salt, coconut cream, scallion, tomato, cucumber and curly dock ribbons and toss gently. Taste for seasoning and adjust as needed. Serve in coconut shell bowls or alongside some coconut rice.

Fresh ahi and curly dock puree ready for marinating.

Mis en place for the Poisson cru: fresh coconut cream, ahi tuna, tomatoes and curly dock

Acorn, Dock and Asian Pear Soup

Acorns, Curly Dock, Asian Pears, Leek, Fenugreek and Whiskey

Serves: 2-4 — Difficulty level: Moderate

Both acorns and curly dock can be a little tannic in different ways, but they still complement each other. The sweetness of the pear and pungent fenugreek make this a woodsy, deeply flavored and satisfying starter. This isn't a difficult soup, but the acorn prep is a step that most likely you'll have to do in advance.

4 cups (120 g) curly dock leaves, washed and stemmed

1 tbsp (15 ml) olive oil

1 small leek, cleaned and finely chopped

1 tsp sea salt, divided

1 tbsp (2 g) dried fenugreek leaves

1 clove garlic, minced

2 cups (480 ml) vegetable stock

1 tsp oaky whiskey

1 dried bay leaf

1 cup (120 g) acorns, leached and skinned (see page 206 for instructions)

1 small Asian pear, peeled and cut into ¼-inch (6-mm) cubes

In a medium pot over medium-high heat, blanch the curly dock in lightly salted boiling water for 2 to 3 minutes. Drain and set aside.

Heat the oil in a medium saucepan over medium heat. Add the leek, ½ teaspoon of the salt and the fenugreek leaves and cook until the leeks become translucent, about 5 to 7 minutes. Add the garlic and cook for 1 more minute. Add the vegetable stock, whiskey, the remaining ½ teaspoon salt, bay leaf, acorns and Asian pear. Bring the soup to a simmer and cook for 20 minutes. You want to soften the acorns a bit. Add the curly dock and cook for another 10 minutes.

Remove the bay leaf and puree the soup with an immersion or high speed blender until smooth. You can strain it to refine the dish and remove any tough particles from the acorns and fenugreek, if desired. Taste for seasoning and adjust as needed.

I serve this with some forbidden rice, vegan zucchini arancini and a dollop of crème fraîche.

Oladi with *Curly Dock* and Friends

Serves: 4 — Difficulty level: Easy

This is more of an inspiration than a recipe and it's a good way for you to explore the complex flavor of curly dock. Another dish for entertaining, this dish also illustrates that you don't have to overthink what to do with your forages. I often feel that's what creates a culinary mind block. I wanted to make a simple dish that showcases the actual flavor of the plant. Here are all the things I think really go with dock:

— Quail eggs and caviar

— Apples dipped in honey with blue cheese

— Cucumbers, tarragon and crème fraîche

— Any kind of dairy product and cheese

From here, you can begin to create your own dishes with some of these flavor profiles. I made some *oladi*, which are like *blinis*, but a little puffier. These are the kind I remember my family making. I guess they are a little more rustic and home-style than blinis. You can use these as a vehicle for mixing and matching flavors with the curly dock, or simply use crackers and explore.

1½ cups (188 g) plus 2 tbsp (16 g) plus 2 tsp (5 g) all-purpose flour

1½ tsp (5 g) active dry yeast

1 tsp sugar

½ tsp sea salt

1 cup (240 ml) of buttermilk, warmed to about 90°F (32°C)

1 large egg, beaten

2 tbsp (30 ml) melted butter, plus more as needed

2 tbsp (30 ml) vegetable oil, plus more as needed

In a food processor fitted with the dough blade, pulse the flour, yeast, sugar and salt to combine. Add the buttermilk and process to combine for 1 minute. Cover the food processor and let the dough mixture sit for 30 minutes. It should double in size. Add the egg and butter and pulse until just combined. Let this rest for another 20 to 30 minutes. While the batter is resting, heat the oil in a large griddle or nonstick pan over medium heat.

The batter should be pretty wet and sticky. Have a spoon ready in a cup of warm water. Dip the spoon in the water, scoop the batter (about 2 tablespoons [30 ml]) and drop it onto the griddle. You may want to shape it with the back of the spoon a bit. You can probably cook 2 to 3 oladi at a time, brushing the pan with additional oil for each batch.

Brush the oladi with additional butter and top with your beautiful wild sorrel (curly dock) and "friends."

Chapter Seven

Lambsquarters

It Does Taste Like Spinach

They know, they just know where to grow, how to dupe you, and how to
camouflage themselves among the perfectly respectable plants, they just
know, and therefore, I've concluded weeds must have brains.

– Dianne Benson, *Dirt*

The genus *Chenopodium* literally means "goosefoot" in Latin, and the leaves do resemble webbed goose feet. When doing your research, you may notice that the family in some sources is Chenopodiaceae and sometimes Amaranthaceae. From time to time, the scholars that be will decide to consolidate or change a family based on new research. As of this writing, it's my understanding that Chenopodiaceae is now considered a subfamily of Amaranthceae. Also, you may see lambsquarters spelled "lambs quarters." American English consolidates the words, while British English separates them.

Chenopodium is both introduced to (via Europe) and naturalized in North America. The most common species found in my area is *album*, or white goosefoot. It's also heavily cultivated in India, Eurasia and parts of Africa, among other places. It's another global green that's eaten in so many parts of the world, which makes it a little strange, to me, that you seldom hear about this plant other than among serious gardeners (who, most likely, are trying to control it from taking over, understandably), permaculture people or foragers. I have seen it more and more at farmers' markets in recent years, however.

In my area, we also see another species *Chenopodium berlandieri* (also called pigweed), which is found in other states as well. There are many common names for lambsquarters, including goosefoot, fat-hen, Belgian spinach and wild spinach. Because it is such a common weed worldwide, the local and regional names have become ambiguous, so it's still important to do some taxonomy and be able to use several identifiers for a 100-percent positive identification.

Lambsquarters (*Chenopodium album*)

Lambsquarters

Chenopodium album
Amaranthaceae family
Introduced, naturalized

Flavor Profile

I've probably mentioned that many people say a lot of forages taste like spinach. I often disagree, but in this case, I must admit, lambsquarters do taste like spinach with some distinguishing characteristics. Spinach, amaranth, beets and quinoa are also in the Amaranthaceae family, after all. Store-bought spinach has a very strong mineral quality with a slightly metallic or iron-rich aftertaste that can be a little tannic. Fresh, young lambsquarters have all the deep green flavor minus that metallic aftertaste. The young seeds have a faint, raw sesame-like taste. As the plant gets older (and especially if the plant is growing in really dry conditions), it produces and accumulates oxalic acid, and it can get bitter and the leaves can get tough. In addition, lambsquarters contain high amounts of oxalic acid and calcium, both of which have been purported to lead to kidney stones and possibly rheumatoid arthritis, among other conditions. This also applies to your average spinach and kale, however, so eating them raw in moderation is key.

You'll notice I tend to blanch almost all my wild greens if I'm going to eat them on a semiregular basis. The cooking and blanching in combination with other foods, like dairy or lemon juice, can break down those acids and crystals. Like nettles, lambsquarters stay a vibrant although slightly darker green during the cooking process. If I'm making a broth, I'll also cook lambsquarters in a nonreactive pan or pot to avoid oxidizing or turning the liquid dark.

To me, this isn't a bland, ubiquitous green but has definite flavor affinities which we'll explore. It's earthy and musty in a good way. When cooked, it has a much more pronounced spinach flavor than spinach. It lends itself to both bright and rich flavors. It can definitely substitute spinach or chard.

Lambsquarters (*Chenopodium album*)

Hybrid variety of lambsquarters

When and How to Harvest

Lambsquarters will shoot up anywhere from very early spring after the frosts die down to late summer before they go to seed in the fall. It's not uncommon to see them all year round near well-watered areas in temperate climates. When you harvest, take from the top third of the plant, following your honorable harvesting protocol. You can use the seeds as you would quinoa. Like quinoa, they can be very bitter and I usually blanch and toast them before using.

Lambsquarters likes to grow in such a variety of places, including fields, wooded areas, roadsides, gardens and any disturbed soils. It's one of those plants you often see growing through sidewalk cracks (although I don't suggest harvesting from this source) as well as sporadically throughout the garden. If you don't want this to spread in your garden, definitely harvest it before it goes to seed.

Distinguishing Identifiers

- Top leaves are smaller and more of a diamond shape than the lower goosefoot-shaped leaves on young plants

- Goosefoot-shaped leaves on mature plants

- Powdery coating on leaves

- Seed-like flowers

- Smells like spinach when crushed

Possible Look-Alikes

- **Nightshade** (toxic)

Lambsquarters Clouds

Egg Soufflé with Lambsquarters

Serves: 2 — Difficulty Level: Easy

I put this dish in the "dishes for entertaining" category because it's almost too pretty to eat. The best thing is that it's so incredibly easy. It's an egg white soufflé with a vibrant, rich, spinach-like base, creamy egg yolk and a chunk of melty Camembert cheese. It's basically another take on baked eggs in cream, which I love and used to make before this recipe came along. This is a little lighter and surprisingly less fussy. It's a no-waste recipe, too. It's one egg per person, both the whites and yolks. You can make individual servings as I do or use a larger ramekin and share it family-style.

3 cups (90 g) lambsquarters leaves, washed and stemmed

2 tbsp (30 ml) heavy cream

2 pinches sea salt, divided

White pepper, to taste

1 tsp fresh chives, finely chopped

2 large eggs, separated and at room temperature

1 tbsp (14 g) butter, divided

1 tbsp (10 g) Camembert, divided

Preheat the oven to 400°F (204°C).

In a medium stockpot over high heat, blanch the lambsquarters in salted boiling water for 2 to 3 minutes to release any bitter flavors and soften the leaves for blending. Drain and gently wring them dry in a clean kitchen towel. In a small blender (or using an immersion blender in medium bowl), blend the lambsquarters with the cream, a pinch of the salt, the white pepper and chives until smooth (a few chunks are perfectly fine). Set aside.

With a hand mixer or in a small stand mixer, beat the egg whites until stiff peaks form, 3 to 5 minutes. Be careful not to overbeat them to the dry and crumbly stage, or they will collapse in the oven. Transfer the egg whites to a pastry bag with a fitted tip and set aside. Or you can use a quart zip-top bag and fashion a pastry bag by snipping off a small portion of one the corners and pipe through the hole.

Using ½ tablespoon (7 g) of the butter, prepare 2 (4-ounce [120-ml]) ramekins or you can also use buttered paper liners as I've done here.

Assemble the dish by placing ½ tablespoon (5 g) of the Camembert at the bottom of each ramekin, followed by the egg yolk, the remaining pinch salt and half the lambsquarters mixture in each ramekin. Pipe the egg white mixture on top in a little tower, making sure you cover the contents of each ramekin.

Bake for 5 to 6 minutes on the middle oven rack or until browned on top. You may want to watch this, as the top can get browned rather quickly.

Velvety Lambsquarters Potage Soup

Velvety Lambsquarters Soup with Cornmilk

Serves: 6–8 — Difficulty level: Moderate

This was one of the first things I ever made with lambsquarters, and it is still something I make
at least once every season. It's a simple soup that anyone can make, but it's rich and complex and can accompany
a great variety of flavors. It's a wonderful wild-food dish that uses more than one part of the plant.

2 medium starchy potatoes, peeled and cut into 2-inch (6-cm) cubes

1 large or 2 small celery roots, peeled and cut into 2-inch (6-cm) cubes

2 large dried bay leaves

½ tsp black peppercorns

1 tsp sea salt, divided, plus more to taste

10 cups (300 g) lambsquarters leaves, washed and stemmed

2 cups (289 g) fresh corn kernels

2 tbsp (30 ml) olive oil

1 small carrot, peeled and finely chopped

1 large celery stalk, finely chopped

1 large onion, finely chopped

½ tsp white pepper

4–5 cloves garlic confit (page 28)

½ cup (120 ml) dry Spanish sherry

Lambsquarters Seed Cakes (page 158)

Fresh thyme sprigs, for garnish

To a large stockpot over high heat, add the potatoes, celery root, bay leaves, peppercorns, ½ teaspoon of the salt and enough water to cover the vegetables by 1 inch (3 cm). Bring the vegetables to a boil, then reduce the heat to medium-low and simmer for 10–12 minutes or until the celery root is tender. Remove the vegetables and set aside. Reserve 6 cups (1.4 L) of the cooking water. Discard the bay leaves and peppercorns. In a non-reactive medium stockpot over medium-high heat, blanch the lambsquarters leaves in lightly salted boiling water for 2 to 3 minutes. Drain and set aside.

Add the corn kernels to a small food processor and pour 1 cup (240 ml) very hot water over them. Pulse the hot water and corn for a few minutes to release the liquid and starch from the kernels. Strain the puree into a sieve over a small bowl and press a spoon against the corn to get all the liquid into the bowl. You should have about 1 cup (240 ml) of corn "milk." Set aside. Heat the oil in a large sauté pan over medium heat. Add the carrot, celery, onion, remaining ½ teaspoon salt and white pepper until the onion is translucent and soft, about 5 to 7 minutes.

In a large food processor or blender (or using an immersion blender), combine 4 cups (960 ml) of the vegetable-cooking water, the potatoes and celery root, sautéed vegetable mixture and lambsquarters. Blend until smooth. Add the garlic confit cloves, sherry and corn puree another 2 to 3 minutes. Add salt to taste. If the soup needs more liquid, add more of the vegetable-cooking water.

Transfer the soup to a large pot over medium high heat, bring to a simmer and cook for 6 to 7 minutes to cook off the raw alcohol flavor. Strain the soup for a more velvety texture. Serve the soup with a beautiful swirl of the corn milk along with some crisp Lambsquarters Seed Cakes and garnish with some fresh thyme.

A Dip on the *Wilder* Side

Smoky Lambsquarters, Wild Herring and White Bean Dip

Serves: 4 — Difficulty level: Easy

Spinach dip is a beloved favorite and many people make that dish with lambsquarters. It's fun, easy and really satisfying. This particular recipe is equally as easy but also dressed up a bit. I make this or dishes like this when it's just too hot to cook. During the hottest months, I'll have homemade cooked beans, legumes and grains on hand so I can easily toss them into a cold salad. And sometimes, if I don't have cooked beans on hand, I'm not above using high-quality, organic, BPA-free canned beans from the market. Here I use them to make a dip that's really a meal in itself.

I also happen to have a hand smoker. It's a small, affordable and very handy tool you can use to infuse just about anything with a natural smoky flavor. You can smoke something in a zip-top bag or a mason jar. You just feed the machine a few tiny chips of smoking wood while the battery-powered vacuum sucks air in toward the ignited chip embers. With the addition of a lighter, you can smoke foods in just a few minutes. I smoked the raw lambsquarters and let them sit in the smoke for 10 minutes. You can also do this to dried lambsquarters.

1 tbsp (15 ml) olive oil

1 medium shallot, minced

⅛ tsp plus pinch sea salt, divided

1 clove garlic, minced

6 cups (180 g) smoked raw lambsquarters leaves, washed and stemmed

1 (15-oz [425-g]) can butter beans, cannellini beans or great Northern beans, drained and rinsed

¼ cup (60 ml) vegetable broth

1 tbsp (5 g) roughly chopped fresh thyme leaves

1 tbsp (5 g) roughly chopped fresh tarragon

4 oz (100 g) boneless tinned or jarred herring, smoked or unsmoked and packed in oil, drained

2 tbsp (15 g) sour cream

2 medium yellow tomatoes, cut into ¼-inch (6-mm) cubes

¼ medium red onion, finely chopped

Heat the oil in a medium sauté pan over medium-high heat. Add the shallot and the pinch of salt. Sauté until the shallots are translucent, about 5 to 7 minutes, then add the garlic and smoked lambsquarters leaves and cook for another 2 minutes. Remove from the heat.

In a small blender or food processor, pulse the beans with half of the cooked lambsquarters mixture, the vegetable broth, thyme, tarragon and remaining ⅛ teaspoon salt until the mixture is smooth and the consistency of hummus or refried beans. Fold in the remaining half of the lambsquarters mixture.

In a small bowl, crumble the herring into small chunks and set aside.

In a medium serving bowl, assemble the dip by layering the beans, lambsquarters, herring, sour cream, tomatoes and onion. I serve this dip with homemade olive oil crackers and a drizzle of olive oil. It's a nice lazy-day supper.

*See photo on page 148.

Lambsquarters "Master Sauce"

All-Purpose Lambsquarters Sauce

Makes: about 2 cups (480 ml) — **Difficulty level:** Easy

I make this sauce often during lambsquarters season. Sometimes I don't know what I'm going to make, but if I have this sauce handy, I can build an easy dish around it. For the quickest lunch ever, I'll make some stovetop flatbreads, add a drizzle of this sauce and some sliced artisan cheese with herbs and flash it under the broiler. This sauce is a little like a mild green ketchup.

8 cups (240 g) densely packed lambsquarters, washed and stemmed

½ medium shallot, roughly chopped

2 cloves garlic confit (page 28)

1 tbsp (15 ml) apple cider vinegar

1 tbsp (5 g) finely chopped fresh thyme

1 tbsp (5 g) finely chopped fresh parsley

½ cup (120 ml) white wine or sherry

1 cup (240 ml) vegetable stock

⅛ tsp ground nutmeg

½ tsp sea salt

½ tsp sugar

⅛ tsp white pepper

1 tbsp (15 ml) olive oil

¼ tsp lecithin powder

Pinch xanthan gum

In a medium stockpot over medium-high heat, blanch the lambsquarters in lightly salted boiling water for 3 to 4 minutes and, with a slotted spoon, transfer them directly to a high-speed blender. Add the shallot, garlic confit, vinegar, thyme, parsley, wine, stock, nutmeg, salt, sugar and pepper to the blender and blend until very smooth. Strain the mixture and transfer it to a small pot. Bring to a simmer and cook 10 minutes to cook the raw wine and shallot flavors out.

Turn the heat off and add the olive oil. Use an immersion blender to incorporate it all the way. Add the lecithin and xanthan gum and blend for 1 more minute. Taste the sauce for seasoning and adjust as needed. Pour the sauce into an airtight container (like a mason jar) and let it cool all the way. Store in the refrigerator for up to 4 days.

Lambsquarters Seed Cakes

Savory Pan-Seared Cakes of Lambsquarters Seeds, Herbs de Provence and Vegetables

Makes about 12 (1½-inch [4-cm]) cakes — Difficulty level: Easy

This is a very simple recipe that can be made with just a few on-hand pantry items. You can harvest the lambsquarters seeds (and nettle seeds, as well) several ways. You can run your hand along the stalk when the seeds are quite dry and let them fall into a bag. If the seeds are not completely dry and are still green (which I prefer), you can snip a few of the heavy, seed-laden stalks from near the top of the plant. After collecting the stalks, rub them gently between your hands, over a bowl, to release the seeds from the stalks. Once you've removed a majority of the seeds from the stalks, shake them through a medium-fine strainer onto a baking sheet and either dehydrate them at 100°F (38°C) for 4 to 5 hours or dry them in the oven (with the door cracked open) at 200°F (93°C) for 5 to 6 hours. A few seeds go a long way.

2 cups (96 g) dried lambsquarters seeds

4 tbsp (56 g) butter, divided

2 tbsp (30 ml) olive oil, divided

½ medium carrot, finely chopped

1 medium shallot, minced

1 small celery stalk, finely chopped

1 tsp dried herbs de Provence (or any dried herbs of your choice)

1 clove garlic, minced

¼ cup (60 ml) white wine

1 large egg white

¾ cup (81 g) panko breadcrumbs, plus more as needed

¼ cup (25 g) grated Parmesan

In a small stockpot over medium-high heat, bring lightly salted water to a gentle boil and cook the lambsquarters seeds for 10 minutes. The water will release tannins and acids and turn the water a dark yellow. Strain the seeds through a fine-mesh strainer and discard the cooking liquid. The seeds will have opened up a bit and will be softer. Set aside.

In a medium sauté pan over medium heat, add 2 tablespoons (28 g) of the butter and 1 tablespoon (15 ml) of the oil and sauté the carrot, shallot and celery until the vegetables are soft and the shallots are translucent, about 5 to 7 minutes. Add the herbs de Provence and garlic and cook another 2 minutes. Add the lambsquarters seeds and wine and cook another 2 to 3 minutes or until most of the liquid has evaporated or reduced. Transfer the mixture to a medium bowl and let it cool.

Once the mixture has cooled, add the egg white and mix thoroughly. Add the breadcrumbs (they will absorb most of the moisture from the egg). Mix in the Parmesan and fold until just combined. The mixture should be a little sticky and hold together when you form a little ball. If it's too wet, add more breadcrumbs. If it's too dry, add water, ½ teaspoon at a time, until the mixture just comes together.

On a medium baking sheet lined with parchment paper, roll 12 small balls. To flatten the top and bottom, form a circle with your forefinger and thumb. Fit the ball inside and slightly squeeze until secure. With your other hand, gently flatten the tops and bottoms of the balls. They should be about 1 inch (3 cm) thick. Cover the flattened balls with plastic wrap and chill them in the refrigerator for at least 2 hours or up to overnight.

When you are ready to cook to seed cakes, heat the remaining 2 tablespoons (28 g) butter and 1 tablespoon (15 ml) oil in a medium sauté pan over medium-high heat. Fry the seed cakes 1 to 2 minutes (or until brown) on each side. Once they are brown on the top and bottom, gently turn them on their sides and roll them to brown the sides.

Preheat the oven to 350°F (177°C) while the seed cakes are frying. Place the cooked seed cakes back on the lined baking sheet and bake them in the oven for 10 minutes to cook the insides. Serve the seed cakes hot with some crème fraîche, alongside eggs as a "hash brown" or with some velverty Lambsquarters Potage Soup (page 154).

e-stemming lambsquarter leaves

Remove the lambsquarters seeds from the stalks by rubbing them gently between your hands.

Sieve the seeds to remove any stems and fine leaves before dehydrating.

ehydrated lambsquarters seeds ready for use

Blanched lambsquarters seeds

Finished seed cake

Sarson ka Saag with *Lambsquarters* and *Mustard* Greens

Fragrantly Spiced Lambsquarters and Mustard Leaves in a Curried Crust

Serves: 4-6 — Difficulty level: Moderate

In some parts of India, namely the Punjab region, both lambsquarters and mustard greens are a frequent table vegetable. This dish is a fragrant, quick-cooking dish that can be eaten simply, on top of some stewed lentils. I've made this into handpies with a slightly spicy, curried crust.

FILLING

6 cups (180 g) densely packed mustard leaves, washed and stemmed

6 cups (180 g) densely packed lambsquarters leaves, washed and stemmed

1 tsp cumin seeds

½ tsp coriander seeds

2 tbsp (30 ml) vegetable oil

1 small onion, finely chopped

½ tsp sea salt

1 tbsp (2 g) dried fenugreek leaves

¼ tsp asafoetida, optional

1 tbsp (6 g) grated fresh ginger

4 cloves garlic, minced

2 medium tomatoes, quartered and seeded

1 medium jalapeño, seeds and ribs removed, minced

FILLING

In a medium, non-reactive pot over medium-high heat, blanch the mustard greens and lambsquarters in lightly salted boiling water for 3 to 4 minutes. Drain well and wring the greens slightly with a clean kitchen towel to remove the moisture. Add them to a food processor.

In a medium sautè pan over medium heat, add the cumin and coriander seeds to the dry pan and let them pop, 2 to 3 minutes. Immediately add the oil, onion, salt, fenugreek leaves, asafoetida and ginger and cook until the onion is soft, 5 to 6 minutes. Add the garlic, tomatoes and jalapeño and cook another 2 to 3 minutes or until most of the liquid has evaporated. Remove from the heat.

Let the filling cool down and add it to the food processor with the lambsquarters and mustard leaves. Pulse a few times for a chunky texture. Transfer the mixture to a small bowl, cover and store in the refrigerator until you are ready to assemble the handpies.

(continued)

CURRIED PIE CRUST

1½ cups (188 g) all-purpose flour

½ tsp sea salt

1 tbsp (6 g) curry powder

8 tbsp (112 g) cold butter, cubed

2 large eggs, divided

6 tbsp (90 ml) ice water, divided

10–12 (1-inch [3-cm]) paneer cheese cubes, optional

CURRIED PIE CRUST

To a food processor fitted with the dough blade, add the flour, salt and curry powder and pulse to aerate, sift and blend the mixture. Add the butter in 4 increments, pulsing until you have pea-size chunks of butter distributed throughout the flour.

Separate 1 of the eggs. Reserve the egg white in a small, airtight container and place it in the refrigerator until you're ready to fill the handpies. Mix the egg yolk with 4 tablespoons (60 ml) of the ice water. With the processor running, slowly add the ice water–egg mixture 1 tablespoon (15 ml) at a time. If the dough comes together in a slightly sticky ball, you can stop, but if it's a bit crumbly, slowly add the remaining 2 tablespoons (30 ml) ice water. Divide the dough in two, form into discs, wrap each one tightly with plastic wrap and refrigerate for 8 hours or up to overnight.

Preheat the oven to 350°F (177°C).

When you are ready to make the handpies, divide each disc of dough into 5 to 6 balls and, on a lightly floured work surface, roll them out to about ⅛-inch (3-mm) thick circles. Divide the filling into about 10 to 12 equal portions.

Lightly brush the inside centers of one side of the dough circles with the reserved egg white so the filling doesn't make the dough soggy. Fill the dough circles with 1 cube of paneer (if using) and 1 portion of the filling. Fold each piece of dough into a half-circle, stretching the dough slightly to seal the handpie. Use the back of a fork to press the edges together. Beat the remaining egg in a small bowl to form an egg wash and brush it on the tops of the handpies before baking.

Bake the handpies on a large baking sheet lined with parchment paper for 20 to 25 minutes or until slightly browned.

Serve the handpies warm with some spiced and herbed yogurt or spicy pickled chilies and onions.

Lambsquarters Marbled Bread

Bread baked with Lambsquarters and Lambsquarters seeds

Makes: 1 (1-lb [455-g]) loaf — Difficulty level: Advanced

Although I tend to bake a lot, now that I think of it, I'm not a baker per se. But I do love Asian-style breads for their soft pillowy texture. I would often admire this super-light bread from afar, but then I discovered how easy it is to make. You can make this bread in a food processor and the only trick is the milk roux starter. You can color and flavor the bread with whatever you'd like. I often make this bread with squid ink for a velvety, intensely black pullman loaf, but I will make this with pureed lambsquarters or nettles and their seeds if I have an abundance of either. These kinds of breads make wonderful savory French toast.

BREAD ROUX

½ cup (120 ml) water

½ cup (120 ml) milk

⅓ cup (42 g) bread flour

MARBLED BREAD

2 tbsp (6 g) lambsquarters seeds

2 cups (60 g) lambsquarters leaves, washed and stemmed

½ cup (120 ml) milk, warmed to 110°F (43°C), divided

2½ cups (312 g) bread flour, divided

¼ cup (48 g) sugar, divided

1 tsp sea salt, divided

2¼ tsp (7 g) active dry yeast, divided

2 large eggs, beaten, divided

4 tbsp (56 g) butter, softened, divided

Note: For this bread, I use a standard *pain de mie*–style or pullman-style loaf pan, which measures 9 x 4 x 4 inches (23 x 10 x 10 cm).

BREAD ROUX

In a small saucepan over medium-high heat, bring the water and milk to a simmer until just scalded. Turn the heat down to low and quickly whisk in the flour until the mixture tightens up to the consistency of thick pudding, about 1 to 2 minutes. Remove the saucepan from the heat and immediately transfer the flour mixture to a small bowl to cool. Cover the bowl with plastic wrap to prevent the mixture forming a skin on top. Let this mixture cool completely.

MARBLED BREAD

Blanch, dehydrate and toast the lambsquarters seeds according to the directions on page 158 and set aside.

In a medium, non-reactive pot over medium-high heat, blanch the lambsquarters leaves in lightly salted boiling water for 3 to 4 minutes. Drain well.

In a food processor fitted with the S blade or bread blade, process ¼ cup (60 ml) of the milk with the lambsquarters until very smooth. Transfer the mixture to a small bowl, cover the bowl and keep warm.

Remove the S blade from the processor and replace it with the dough blade. Add 1¼ cups (156 g) of the flour, ⅛ cup (24 g) of the sugar, ½ teaspoon of the salt and 1⅛ teaspoons (3.5 g) of the yeast and pulse to blend thoroughly, about 2 to 3 minutes.

Add half of 1 of the beaten eggs, half the milk roux and all the lambsquarters puree and process for 5 minutes on medium speed or the knead function. Add 2 tablespoons (28 g) of the butter and process for another 5 minutes. Transfer the dough to an oiled bowl to rise for 1 hour or until doubled in size. Cover the bowl with an oiled piece of plastic wrap.

(continued)

Lambsquarters puree dough and lambsquarters seed dough

The doughs rolled one on top of the other to create a marbled effect

To make the lighter colored dough, repeat this process using the remaining 1¼ cups (156 g) flour, ⅛ cup (24 g) sugar, ½ teaspoon salt and 1⅛ teaspoons (3.5 g) yeast. Add the lambsquarters seeds to the flour mixture and process. Add the remaining ¼ cup (60 ml) milk, the remaining half of 1 of the beaten eggs and the remaining half of the milk roux and process. Finally, add the remaining 2 tablespoons (14 g) butter and process. Transfer this to another oiled bowl, cover the bowl with oiled plastic wrap and let the dough rise for 1 hour or until doubled. Because the half with the lambsquarters puree is denser, it will be a little smaller after the rise.

After the doughs have doubled in size, punch them down and transfer them to a floured work surface. Make 2 logs a little shorter than the length of your loaf pan. Place one on top of the other and press down. With a floured rolling pin, roll lengthwise to flatten and then begin rolling crosswise until you have a rough square. Like you would a jelly roll, roll the dough in on itself back into a log the length of the bread pan. Line the bottom of the pan with parchment paper and oil the bottom and sides. Carefully place the dough inside the bread pan and score the top with a sharp knife. Let this rise a second time for about 45 minutes somewhere warm and free of drafts. You can tent it with aluminum foil, leaving enough room to it rise.

Preheat the oven to 350°F (177°C).

In a small bowl, combine the remaining beaten egg with 1 teaspoon water. Mix well and carefully brush the top of the loaf with the egg wash, being careful not to deflate it. Sprinkle some coarse salt on top or extra lambsquarters seeds if you have them. Place the loaf pan on a medium baking sheet and bake 30 to 35 minutes or until browned. When the pan is cool enough to handle, turn the bread out onto a cooling rack. It should come out easily, but if the egg wash touched the side of the pan, it may stick. Just use a sharp paring knife to loosen. Once the bread has cooled, store it in an airtight container. It keeps remarkably well for up to 5 days. It also freezes really well.

Lambsquarters Marbled Bread Savory French Toast

Marbled Lambsquarters Bread, Herbs and Sharp Cheese

Serves: 4 — Difficulty level: Easy

4 large eggs, beaten

4 tbsp (60 ml) heavy cream

½ tsp sea salt

Pinch white pepper

2 tbsp (10 g) finely chopped fresh thyme leaves

2 tbsp (10 g) finely grated hard cheese, such as Pecorino Romano or Parmesan, divided

4 (1-inch [3-cm] thick) slices Lambsquarters Marbled Bread (page 163)

2 tbsp (30 ml) olive oil, divided

2 tbsp (28 g) butter, divided

Preheat the oven to 200°F (93°C).

In a 2-quart (2-L) rectangular baking dish, beat the eggs and add the cream, salt, white pepper, thyme and and half of the cheese and combine well. Cut the bread into triangles. Soak the bread pieces in the egg mixture for 1 minute on each side. Lift each piece with a slotted spoon to drain off the excess liquid before placing the bread in a sauté pan.

Heat 1 tablespoon (15 ml) of the oil and 1 tablespoon (14 g) of the butter in a large sauté pan over medium heat. Swirl the pan to combine. Lay half the drained toast pieces in the pan and sprinkle 1 teaspoon of the cheese of the tops of this batch. Cook for 3 to 4 minutes and then flip the bread and cook the other side for 3 to 4 minutes to toast the cheese. Repeat this process until you've finished cooking all the French toast. Hold the toast in the oven on a heat-proof plate covered with aluminum foil until ready to serve.

Sprinkle the French toast with the remainder of the cheese. Serve with lots of bacon and some thick slices of ripe tomatoes.

Sweet and Sour Lambsquarters and Eggplant Gimbap

Seaweed-Wrapped Lambsquarters, Eggplant and Rice

Serves: 4 — Difficulty level: Moderate

As I was looking back on the recipes I've included here, it occurred to me that it's been a really warm spring and exceedingly hot summer. My choices in meals are decidedly lighter and involve as little oven and stove time as possible. This recipe is a really fun one for kids and adults alike. *Gimbap* are basically rice balls stuffed with something delicious and then wrapped in seaweed. I live by some fantastic Asian markets and they sell a variety of gimbap wrappers. If you are not familiar with them, they are usually nori sheets lined on both sides with plastic wrap. You fold the wraps, plastic and all, around your rice ball (well, it's more like a triangle) and seal it with a cute little sticker. When you are ready to eat, you remove the sticker, pull a little tab and presto, like magic, the plastic tears away and you can enjoy your lunch with a fresh, crispy nori wrapper. You can also just wrap the gimbap with nori sheets if you are eating them right away. This dish is sweet, tangy and savory, is perfect at room temperature and is a great way to get some veggies in.

1 cup (200 g) sticky or short-grain rice

6 cups (180 g) densely packed lambsquarters, washed and stemmed

2 small Chinese eggplants, unpeeled and cut into ¼-inch (6-mm) cubes

1 tbsp (15 g) sea salt

2 tbsp (30 ml) olive oil or vegetable oil

½ small red bell pepper, cored and cut into ¼-inch (13-mm) cubes

1 small red Thai chili, optional

2 cloves garlic, minced

1 tsp minced fresh ginger

2 tbsp (31 g) tomato paste

½ tsp sesame oil, plus more if needed

2 tbsp (30 ml) rice wine vinegar

1 tbsp (15 ml) agave

½ tsp cornstarch

2 tbsp (30 ml) tamari

Pinch white pepper

4 (8 x 9-inch [20 x 23-cm]) sheets nori

Chinese bacon, optional, for serving

Fresh cilantro sprouts or leaves, optional, for serving

Sesame seeds, optional, for serving

Pickled ginger, optional, for serving

Cook the rice according to the package's instructions. Transfer the cooked rice to a bowl, cover the bowl and let the rice cool down enough to handle.

In a medium, non-reactive stockpot over medium-high heat, blanch your lambsquarters in lightly salted boiling water for 3 to 4 minutes. Drain and gently pat the lambsquarters dry. Set aside.

In a shallow bowl, sprinkle the eggplant with the salt and toss to combine thoroughly. Let the eggplant sit at room temperature for 30 minutes. The water will leach out, allowing your stir-fry to get a little crispy instead of watery. After 30 minutes, drain and rinse the eggplant really well to remove the salt. Pat it dry firmly to remove any excess water.

(continued)

Sweet and Sour Lambsquarters and Eggplant Gimbap (Cont.)

Heat the oil in a medium saucepan over medium-high heat. Sauté the eggplant and bell pepper until the eggplant is browned, 8 to 10 minutes. Add the Thai chili, garlic and ginger and cook for 1 more minute. In a small bowl, thoroughly mix the tomato paste with the sesame oil and add to the pan and combine well. Add in the lambsquarters and stir.

In the same bowl you mixed the tomato paste, mix the vinegar, agave, cornstarch and tamari until smooth. Add this mixture to the sauté pan along with the white pepper and stir vigorously to combine. Cook for another 2 to 3 minutes. If the mixture becomes too thick, add water, 1 teaspoon at a time. Taste for salt and adjust as needed. Take the sauté pan off the heat and let the mixture cool.

If you are not using rice molds, scoop about ½ cup (48 g) of the cooled, cooked rice onto a 1-foot (30-cm) square piece of plastic wrap and flatten the rice out a little. Place 1 tablespoon (28 g) of the lambsquarter-eggplant mixture in the middle of the rice. Close the plastic around the rice, keeping the mixture in the middle of the ball, and press firmly to pack the rice into a ball. Once it's in a ball shape, form it into a rough triangle and carefully remove the plastic. If the plastic sticks, very lightly oil it with the sesame oil. Be careful when oiling the plastic wrap, because if you add to much oil, the rice won't stick to itself. Wrap each triangle in a sheet of nori and enjoy. Alternatively, you can make a rice bowl and top with the lambsquarters-eggplant mixture, thin strips of nori and the optional Chinese bacon, cilantro, sesame seeds and pickled ginger.

Strawberry and Lambsquarters Fields Forever

Strawberry-Glazed Porkchops with Lambsquarters Stuffing, Wilted Lambsquarters, Garden Basil and Fresh Strawberries

Serves: 4-6 — Difficulty level: Moderate

This is another dish that's company worthy. It's impressive, beautiful, extremely flavorful, memorable and just reminds you of summer. It's a pretty hearty meal (the pork chops are enormous double chops) comprised of the main protein, side and salad all in one. I think this is a wonderful dish served on a platter. The earthiness of the lambsquarters and basil and sweet tartness of the strawberries complement the juicy chops, and the lambsquarters stuffing acts as the meal's rich starch component.

The secret to this dish is to brine the chops. This step almost guarantees a perfect chop, and I always do this with larger pieces of pork. If it seems like a lot of lambsquarters, it is, but when they come into season, they really come into season. If you have a little early summer rain in your future, start thinking about this dish.

12 cups (360 g) densely packed lambsquarters, washed and stemmed, divided

2 large dried bay leaves

2 cloves garlic, smashed

½ large white or brown onion, halved

1 tbsp (5 g) crushed fresh or dried juniper berries, optional

3 tbsp (45 g) sea salt plus ½ tsp, divided

4 (2½-inch [6-cm] thick) double-cut, bone-in pork chops

4 tbsp (56 g) butter, divided

2 tbsp (30 ml) olive oil plus 1 tsp, divided

2 medium shallots, minced

½ medium celery stalk, minced

1 tbsp (5 g) finely chopped fresh thyme leaves

2 cups (140 g) toasted bread cubes

⅛ cup (30 ml) vegetable or chicken stock

1 cup (25 g) densely packed basil leaves, divided

1 large egg white, lightly beaten

4 tbsp (100 g) chunky strawberry jam

1 tbsp (15 ml) good-quality balsamic vinegar

10 large strawberries, sliced into ⅛-inch (3-mm) thick rounds

Freshly ground black pepper, to taste

In a medium, non-reactive stockpot over medium-high heat, blanch 4 cups (120 g) of the lambsquarters in lightly salted boiling water for 3 to 4 minutes. Drain and gently wring them dry.

To a gallon zip-top bag, add 8 to 10 cups (1.9 to 2.4 L) water, the bay leaves, garlic, onion, juniper berries (if using) and 3 tablespoons (45 g) of the salt. Let the salt dissolve. Add the pork chops to the brine, seal the bag (letting as much air out as possible) and let the pork chops sit overnight in the refrigerator (but no more than 12 hours). Rinse them really well to remove the salt, pat them dry and let them come to room temperature before cooking.

(continued)

Preheat your oven broiler. Prepare the stuffing by melting 2 tablespoons (28 g) of the butter with 1 tablespoon (15 ml) of the oil in a medium sauté pan over medium-high heat. Add the shallots, celery, thyme and ¼ teaspoon of the salt and cook until the vegetables are translucent, about 5 to 7 minutes. Add the bread cubes and toss them in the vegetable mixture until well coated. Add the stock and combine until everything is moistened. Remove the sauté pan from the heat and let the stuffing cool.

Finely chop ½ cup (12.5 g) of the basil leaves. When the stuffing is cool, add the chopped basil and mix well. Taste for salt and adjust as needed, then add the egg white and combine thoroughly. Set aside.

Melt the remaining 2 tablespoons (14 g) butter with the jam in a small pot over medium heat. When well combined, take off the heat and set aside.

Make a deep incision opposite the bones of each double chop, but not deep enough to cut through to any of the sides. You're just going to make nice, deep pockets for the stuffing. Divide the dressing into fourths and stuff each pork chop with a portion of stuffing. I also use soaked kitchen twine to secure the chops and prevent the stuffing from spilling out before they go into the oven. Brush the outside of the chops with the remaining 1 tablespoon (15 ml) oil.

In a large heavy-bottomed pan or cast iron pan over high heat, sear both sides of the chops as well as the fat opposite the bone and the bone itself. The chops are not ready to flip if they won't release. Let them sear until they easily release from the pan. Sear all sides for 2 minutes or until browned.

Place the chops on a piece of lightly oiled parchment paper on a large baking sheet and brush the top of the chops with some of the jam glaze. Broil for 3 minutes. Turn the chops over and brush a thick layer of the jam glaze on the other side and let it brown for another 3 minutes or until it is crackling. If you have an instant-read thermometer or meat thermometer, check the internal temperature in the middle where the stuffing and meat mix. The temperature should be 150°F (66°C) and will increase in carry-over temperature to about 155°F (68°C) while the chops are tented with aluminum foil to rest.

Remove the chops from the oven and tent them with aluminum foil for 15 minutes. Brush the chops again with the jam glaze before serving.

Wipe out the pan you used to sear the chops. Heat the pan over medium-high heat and add the remaining 1 teaspoon oil, swirling it around the pan, then add the vinegar. Add the remaining 8 cups (240 g) lambsquarters and the remaining ¼ teaspoon salt and sauté for 1 to 2 minutes or until the lambsquarters are wilted and coated.

Arrange a bed of sautéed lambsquarters on a platter and place the pork chops on top of the lambsquarters. Place any remaining sautéed lambsquarters around the chops. Add the remaining ½ cup (12.5 g) basil leaves, tearing the leaves and scattering them across the chops. Finally, top the chops with the strawberries and freshly cracked black pepper.

Savory Lambsquarters Rice Pudding

Lambsquarters, Rice, Rosemary and Sheep's Milk Cheese

Serves: 6-8 — Difficulty level: Easy

Lambsquarters and rosemary are one of my favorite combinations. The rosemary will absolutely infuse the kitchen. With the addition of fragrant oregano and tangy mizithra cheese, this casserole is filling yet bright against the earthy lambsquarters. This comfort dish is excellent right out of the oven while piping hot, but it's also wonderful at room temperature and perfect for a potluck. It makes great leftovers—if it lasts that long.

2 tbsp (30 ml) olive oil

1 medium onion, finely chopped

½ tsp plus pinch sea salt, divided

1 tbsp (5 g) finely chopped fresh oregano

1 tbsp (5 g) finely chopped fresh rosemary

1 cup (200 g) short-grain starchy rice

3 large eggs

½ cup (120 ml) heavy cream, plus more as needed

½ cup (120 ml) milk

¾ cup (185 g) ricotta

1 tsp fresh lemon juice

White pepper, to taste

6 cups (180 g) densely packed lambsquarters, washed and stemmed

½ cup (50 g) mizithra or feta, divided

3 tbsp (42 g) butter, plus more as needed

Grease a 6-cup (1.4-L) casserole dish with butter and preheat the oven to 375°F (191°C).

Heat the oil in a medium sauté pan over low heat. Add the onions and a pinch of the salt and cook until the onion is very brown, 35 to 45 minutes, stirring occasionally. Add the oregano and rosemary during the last 5 minutes of cooking. In the meantime, cook the rice in very lightly salted water according to the package's instructions. This should take anywhere from 25 to 35 minutes.

In a large mixing bowl, whisk the eggs and then add the cream, milk, ricotta, lemon juice, remaining ½ teaspoon salt and pepper, whisking to combine. Add the lambsquarters, onion, rice and ¼ cup (25 g) of the mizithra and combine well, folding to distribute everything evenly. The mixture should be a little loose, but not soupy. If it absorbs all the liquid, add up to ¼ cup (60 ml) more cream.

Pour the mixture into the greased casserole dish. Sprinkle the remaining ¼ cup (25 g) mizithra on top and dot evenly with the butter.

Bake for 35 to 40 minutes. Check the top to see how brown it is after 20 minutes. If it's browning too quickly, tent the casserole with aluminum foil to prevent burning. Let the casserole cool for at least 15 to 20 minutes before eating to let everything set.

Trippa Finta (Faux Tripe) *Verde*

Cooked Cheese Rinds, Lambsquarters and Tomato Broth

Serves: 4-6 — Difficulty level: Easy

I found this soup recipe in a gorgeous Tuscan cookbook, *Toscana in Cucina: The Flavours of Tuscany*, published by Sime Books. The dish just seemed so clean, understated and focused on the quality of a few ingredients. I loved the idea and have adapted it, making it a bit lighter here. The "tripe" is the unused rind of part of a wheel of Parmigiano-Reggiano that often gets discarded. I asked my cheese monger if she'd sell it to me. She was so happy to and was glad that people are starting to use this again. With fresh lambsquarters, the very best tomatoes and a little wine, this soup is a winner. The texture of the rinds after preparing look uncannily like tripe (which, traditionally, is the stomach tissue of an animal) and is solid but is also melty, chewy, very flavorful and concentrated when warmed by the soup. The broth of wine, lambsquarters and Parmigiano-Reggiano water has so many layers of flavor.

1 (16-oz [455-g]) piece Parmigiano-Reggiano rind

2 tbsp (30 ml) olive oil

2 medium onions, cut into ⅛-inch (3-mm) pieces

½ tsp plus pinch sea salt, divided

4 cups (960 ml) vegetable stock

2 cups (480 ml) dry white wine

3 tbsp (15 g) roughly chopped fresh Italian parsley, divided

1 (14-oz [400-g]) can baby Italian Roma tomatoes, drained

6 cups (180 g) densely packed lambsquarters, washed and stemmed

1 clove garlic, smashed

2 tbsp (60 g) minced pickled piri piri peppers, for garnish

With a very sharp, heavy knife, cut the Parmigiano-Reggiano rind into long 1-inch (3-cm) wide strips.

Bring water to a boil in a large non-reactive stockpot over high heat. When the water is at a rolling boil, add the cheese rind using a spider. Submerge the Parmigiano-Reggiano for 2 minutes to remove any wax and impurities from the rind. Remove and lay it on a slightly oiled plate so it doesn't stick. Discard the water, lightly oil the bottom of the stockpot and bring fresh water to a light simmer over medium-high heat. Add the Parmigiano-Reggiano piece back into the water and let this simmer for 1 hour, stirring occasionally, as it tends to stick to the bottom of the pot.

Meanwhile, heat the olive oil in a medium sauté pan over medium heat. Add the onions with a pinch of salt and cook until the onions are translucent, about 5 to 7 minutes. Set aside. After 1 hour, your rind strips should be done. Carefully remove them from the water using a long spatula or spider. They will be very stretchy. Lay them on a slightly oiled plate to cool. Reserve 2 cups (480 ml) of the cooking water.

To the same stockpot, add the vegetable stock, wine, reserved Parmigiano-Reggiano cooking water, onions, 2 tablespoons (8 g) of the parsley, tomatoes, lambsquarters and garlic. Over medium-high heat, bring this to a light simmer for 30 minutes to cook out the raw wine flavor. Add ¼ teaspoon of the salt and taste. It will reduce a bit and get saltier. If it needs more salt at the end, add the remaining ¼ teaspoon salt. Remove and discard the garlic before serving.

Add a few pieces of the cooked Parmigiano-Reggiano rind to the hot soup and let it melt in for a few minutes before serving. Ladle the hot soup into bowls, ensuring everyone gets some onion, lambsquarters and tomatoes. Sprinkle each bowl with a few pickled piri piri peppers and the remaining 1 tablespoon (4 g) parsley. Serve with fresh crusty bread, good-quality olive oil and crunchy salt.

Boiled cheese rind and lambsquarters ready for use

Boiled cheese rind

Freshly picked lambsquarters seeds

Trippa Finta and lambsquarters soup

Lambsquarters and Salt Cod Croquettes

Salt Cod, Allspice, Pimenton and Tarragon

Serves: 8–10 — Difficulty level: Advanced

This isn't so much a difficult dish as it is one with a lot of steps. The dish itself is a party pleaser and is a harmonious blend of creamy potatoes, mild salt cod and earthy lambsquarters. Lightly infused with allspice and some garden herbs, these croquettes are simple yet complex in flavor.

½ lb (228 g) salt cod

4 cups (120 g) densely packed lambsquarters, washed and stemmed

1½ cups (360 ml) milk

4 cloves garlic, minced

1 medium shallot, minced

4–5 allspice berries

1 dried bay leaf

4 medium waxy potatoes, peeled and cut into ½-inch (13-mm) cubes

2 tbsp (28 g) butter

2 cups plus 2 tbsp (266 g) flour, divided

½ tsp pimenton or sweet paprika

2 tbsp (10 g) finely chopped fresh tarragon

2 cups (216 g) fresh breadcrumbs

2 large eggs plus 2 tbsp (30 ml) water, beaten

Pinch of salt and pepper

Vegetable oil, for frying

Soak the salt cod by covering it by 1 inch (3 cm) of water in a container with a lid in the refrigerator. Soak for 24 hours if the salt cod is frozen or 36 hours if the cod is salt-packed. You will need to change the water at least 3 times during this period. Rinse the soaked salt cod well and pat it dry.

In a medium, non-reactive stockpot over medium-high heat, blanch the lambsquarters in lightly salted boiling water for 2 to 3 minutes. Drain, gently pat dry and set aside. In a medium saucepan over medium heat, bring the cod, milk, garlic, shallot, allspice berries and bay leaf to a gentle simmer for 20 minutes. After 20 minutes, remove the cod, add the potatoes and simmer for another 10 minutes or until the potatoes are tender. Strain and reserve all of the liquid. Using a fork, mash the potatoes in a small bowl with 2 tablespoons (30 ml) of the cooking liquid and set aside.

To make a béchamel sauce, make a ball with the butter and 2 tablespoons (16 g) of the flour and knead it a bit to incorporate the flour into the butter. In a small saucepan over medium heat, melt the ball and, with a wooden spoon, work the paste until it bubbles for about 2 to 3 minutes. Slowly add the reserved cooking liquid and the pimenton and let the sauce thicken for 2 to 3 minutes. Transfer the sauce to a bowl and cover it with plastic wrap until you are ready to use to prevent a skin forming on top of the sauce.

Chop the lambsquarters and tarragon finely and set aside. In a large bowl, flake the fish, add the mashed potatoes, lambsquarters and tarragon and combine well. Add the béchamel sauce and fold everything together. Let this chill, covered in the refrigerator, for at least 4 hours or up to overnight so you will easily be able to form croquettes.

When you are ready to fry the croquettes, get a dredging station ready. Set out three shallow bowls and fill one with the remaining 2 cups (250 g) flour, one with the breadcrumbs and one with the beaten eggs. Add a pinch salt and pepper to the flour and mix well. In a mini deep fryer or small cast iron pot or pan heat your oil to 350°F (177°C). Scoop about a golf ball–size (2.5-cm ball) portion of the chilled croquette mixture and gently roll it into a ball. Elongate it a bit into a football shape for even cooking. Dredge it in the flour first, then in the egg, then in the breadcrumbs, gently shaking off any excess flour, egg or breadcrumbs each time before moving on to the next bowl. Fry the croquettes until brown, 4 to 5 minutes. Don't crowd the fryer or pan—just fry 3 to 4 croquettes at a time.

Lambsquarters Mousse Profiteroles with Spicy Lamb Meatballs

Savory Pastry Puffs, Lambsquarters Mousse and Spiced Lamb Meatballs

Serves: 8–10 — Difficulty level: Advanced

This is a great recipe for entertaining, and the components can be made in advance and assembled the next day. Profiteroles are usually sweet, but they can easily be made savory. I add a spicy lamb meatball to these, but you can omit that if you'd like to make these profiteroles vegetarian. The richness of the lambsquarters mousse, airy puffs and spicy meatballs are wonderful contrasts in the mouth.

PÂTE À CHOUX

½ cup (120 ml) water

3 tbsp (42 g) butter

½ tsp sea salt

4 oz (118 g) all-purpose flour

2 large eggs

1 large egg white

SPICY LAMB MEATBALLS

½ medium onion, finely chopped

½ tsp ground cumin

½ tsp ground coriander

⅛ tsp ground allspice

1 tsp chili paste or 2 ground fresh red chilies

1 tbsp (5 g) finely chopped fresh parsley

1 clove garlic, minced

½ tsp sea salt

1 large egg yolk

2 tbsp (30 ml) heavy cream

½ cup (54 g) dry breadcrumbs

1 lb (455 g) ground lamb

2 tbsp (30 ml) olive oil

LAMBSQUARTERS MOUSSE

4 cups (120 g) densely packed lambsquarters, washed and stemmed

⅓ cup (80 ml) chilled heavy cream, divided

½ tsp powdered gelatin

½ tsp fresh lemon juice

⅛ tsp sea salt

PÂTE À CHOUX

Preheat the oven to 450°F (232°C).

In a small pot over medium-high heat, bring the water, butter and salt to a boil. Remove the pot from the heat, add the flour and stir vigorously with a heat-proof spatula to bring the mixture together. Return the pot to the heat, stir quickly until the mixture pulls away from the sides and bottom of the pot. Transfer the mixture to a food processor while it's still warm but not hot and, with the processor running on low speed, add the eggs and egg white until the mixture is smooth and shiny, about 1 to 2 minutes.

(continued)

Lambsquarters Mousse Profiteroles with Spicy Lamb Meatballs (Cont.)

Load the mixture into a pastry bag with a 1-inch (3-cm) tip (you can also use a zip-top bag with a tiny bit cut out of one corner). On a large baking sheet lined with parchment paper, pipe 2-inch (6-cm) puffs in a swirling circle. Leave about 1 inch (3 cm) between each one as they will grow a bit in the oven. Place the baking sheet on the middle rack in the oven and bake for 10 minutes. Turn the heat down to 350°F (177°C) and bake for another 10 minutes (start checking around 7 minutes to see if they are browning too quickly). Remove the profiteroles from the baking sheet and let them cool. Store them in an airtight container. They can be reheated for 3 to 4 minutes at 350°F (177°C) before serving, but they are also fine at room temperature.

SPICY LAMB MEATBALLS

In a large bowl, combine the onion, cumin, coriander, allspice, chili paste, parsley, garlic, salt, egg yolk, cream and breadcrumbs. Mix thoroughly. Break apart the ground lamb and fold it into the onion. Roll 25 to 30 little meatballs. Heat the oil in a medium cast iron or heavy-bottomed pan over medium-high heat, and fry the meatballs until browned, about 4 to 5 minutes. Tent the pan with aluminum foil and set aside until ready to serve.

LAMBSQUARTERS MOUSSE

In a medium non-reactive stockpot over medium-high heat, blanch the lambsquarters in lightly salted boiling water for 2 to 3 minutes. Drain, let cool and gently wring dry with a kitchen towel. Meanwhile, heat 1 tablespoon (15 ml) of the cream either in a small pot over medium heat, or for 20 to 30 seconds in a microwave on high heat. The cream should reach 110°F (43°C). Add the gelatin to the cream, stirring until it has dissolved. Let the cream cool.

To a food processor, add the lambsquarters, salt, 1 tablespoon (15 ml) of the cream and lemon juice and process until very smooth. In a stand mixer, whip the remaining chilled cream with the bloomed gelatin into stiff peaks. Fold in the lambsquarters mixture gently. Transfer the mixture to a pastry bag with a 1-inch (3-cm) tip and chill for 10 minutes to set.

To serve, remove the little "hats" from the profiteroles, fill with a meatball and then pipe a little bit of the mousse over the meatball. Garnish with some fresh herbs if desired.

Oysters Rockefeller with *Lambsquarters*

Oysters, Chervil, Lambsquarters and Parmesan

Serves: 6 — Difficulty level: Easy

This is a classic that joins the sea and field. Oysters are one of my favorite foods on the planet, and I'm pretty fond of lambsquarters. If you have access to fresh oysters, this is a quick entertaining dish that takes very little effort and time, and you probably have most of the ingredients on hand already.

12 fresh oysters

¾ cup (81 g) panko breadcrumbs

Sea salt and freshly ground black pepper, to taste

6 tbsp (84 g) butter, divided

4 cloves garlic, minced

2 cups (20 g) chervil, washed and roughly chopped

¼ cup (25 g) grated Parmesan

1 tbsp (15 ml) olive oil

6 cups (180 g) densely packed lambsquarters, washed, stemmed and finely chopped

¼ cup (60 ml) white wine

6 cups (500 g) of rock salt, optional

Preheat the oven to 475°F (246°C).

Make sure the oysters are cleaned of all debris on the outside of the shells, that there are no cracked shells and that none of the shells are opened (which means they are dead). Once the oysters are washed and cleaned, carefully shuck them open over a small bowl, saving the liquid. Carefully remove the oysters from the shells with a small paring knife. Keep the oysters in their liquid in the refrigerator until right before cooking. Reserve the shells.

In another small bowl, combine the breadcrumbs and a pinch salt and pepper. In a small sauté pan over medium heat, melt 3 tablespoons (42 g) of the butter and cook the garlic until just fragrant, about 1 to 2 minutes. Pour the butter and garlic over the breadcrumbs, add the chervil and Parmesan and mix.

To the same sauté pan, add the oil, lambsquarters and reserved oyster liquid and wilt the lambsquarters, about 2 minutes. Add the wine and cook for another 3 to 4 minutes, reducing slightly. Set aside.

Line a medium baking sheet with parchment and then top with an even layer of rock salt. This is to keep the oysters upright so they don't lose their liquid and dry out. If you don't have rock salt, you can use aluminum foil, scrunched up, to hold the oysters upright.

Place 1 shucked oyster in each shell and spoon 1 tablespoon (5 g) of the lambsquarters mixture over each oyster, followed by 1 teaspoon of the breadcrumb mixture, patting it into the oyster shells down slightly. Dot the oysters with the remaining 3 tablespoons (42 g) butter and bake for 10 minutes or until brown and bubbling.

Chapter Eight

Elderberry and Elderflowers

A Study in Contrasts

And besides, look at elder-flowers and bluebells—they are a sign that pure
creation takes place—even the butterfly.

– D. H. Lawrence

The regal elder trees are definitely not in the "ugly little greens" category. They are majestic, showy and beautiful. There's definitely an air of excitement and expectation when you see the first snowy flowers of the season, because you know that there will be perfumy cordial and later, lush elderberry wine, among other delicacies. Because the flowers are so astonishing and noticeable, they scream spring and officially herald in the season. There are so many culinary and medicinal uses with this tree, from skin-soothing elderflower hydrosol and flu-fighting elderberry cordial to simple, cooling elderflower infusions. And don't forget the berries—there are so many ways to use the berries with sweet and savory recipes.

Elderberry

Sambucus nigra

Adoxa family

Both introduced and native throughout the United State and large parts of Canada; depending on location, you may see blue, black, red or white elderberries

Red elderberries are considered toxic

Elderberry (*Sambucus*)

a few clusters of the flowers you can make a good quantity of cordial, for example. Where I live, quite a few people have planted the trees as landscape, so it's always near.

Distinguishing Identifiers

- Small, yellowish-white flowers with five petals
- Tripinnate leaves with smooth edges
- Tight, umbrella-shaped berry clusters with ripe berries the size of capers

Possible Look-Alikes

- Dogwood
- **Pokeberry** (toxic)
- **Water hemlock** (the flowers look a little similar, toxic)
- Hercules' club

Flavor Profile

The black elderberry is lush, rich and has a subtle tannic flavor (especially when dried), which pairs well with savory dishes. It is a very full-bodied berry. The white elderberries have more of a white wine–grape quality and lend themselves to sweet preparations. The flowers are heady, perfumy and floral with a hint of vanilla. There is nothing that smells like them. A unique scent, it is subtle and powerful at the same time.

When and How to Harvest

Almost every region has microclimates, so you may see elderflowers bloom anywhere from early spring to early fall. And you might see flowers at the same time as ripe berries. There's a short window for both the flowers and berries. Take only what you need. A little of both goes a long way. With just

Elderflower Cordial

Fragrant Nonalcoholic Elderflower Syrup

Makes: about 10 cups (2.4 L) — **Difficulty level:** Easy

Elderflower cordial is the base and very building block of cooking and infusing foods with elderflowers. It can be added to rich creams and butters for delicate desserts, as well as savory sauces and seafood dishes. It's also indispensable when making cocktails. I've adapted from *The New Wildcrafted Cuisine: Exploring the Exotic Gastronomy of Local Terroir* by Pascal Baudar.

4 cups (152 g) elderflowers, stemmed

6 cups (1.4 L) distilled water

3 large lemons, sliced into ⅛-inch (3-mm) thick rounds

5 cups (1 kg) sugar

1½ tsp (7 g) citric acid

Place the elderflowers in a large bowl or basket and leave it outside, preferably overnight. There are little black bugs that love to hide inside the flowers. Putting the flowers outside will allow them to migrate away. Don't wash the flowers. The pollen that clings to the flowers is what makes the magical elderflower aroma and flavor.

Over a clean bowl, lightly pluck at the flowers with your hands and let the little florets fall into the bowl along with the pollen. Take care to remove any stems as they can be slightly toxic.

In a large stockpot over high heat, bring the water, lemons and sugar to a boil for 15 minutes. Take the stockpot off the heat, add the citric acid and elderflowers and stir well to combine. Transfer the mixture to a large heat-proof container with a lid to cool and release all the flavors (at least 24 hours up to 48 hours). Once the liquid has cooled completely, you can strain the liquid through several layers of cheesecloth, squeezing out as much liquid from the flowers and lemons as you can. At this point, you can store the cordial in mason jars or other airtight containers in the refrigerator or water-bath can them for future use. There are many preservation books that go into detail, but basically, it's transferring the liquid to sterilized canning jars (leaving 1 inch [3 cm] of room from the top), lidding the jars and then water-bath canning for 20 minutes. You should hear the seal pop after removing the jars from the water to know it's airtight. You'll need a simple water-bath canning kit, which includes the pot, a jar rack, jar tongs, jar filter and funnel.

Elderberry Braised Pot Roast

Beef, Elderberries and Wine

Serves: 4-6 — Difficulty level: Moderate

This is a wonderful dish for a slow cooker, but since I don't own one, the stovetop and oven work just as well. It's a hefty dish with tons of flavor and perfect for a lazy Sunday supper. You can make this with fresh or frozen elderberries. You can also make it with dried berries, but if you do, use three-fourths the amount listed below, as dried elderberries are more concentrated than fresh or frozen. Dried elderberries have a deeper and more tannic flavor than fresh and the cooking liquid will be darker.

4 lb (1.8 kg) chuck roast, cleaned, trimmed of any silver skin

4 tbsp (60 ml) olive oil, divided

2 tbsp (30 g) plus 1 tsp sea salt, divided

1 tsp freshly ground black pepper

1 large onion, peeled and halved

2 cloves garlic, roughly chopped

4 cups (360 g) elderberries, washed and stemmed

½ cup (120 ml) red wine vinegar

½ cup (120 ml) port wine, optional

6 cups (1.4 L) beef stock, vegetable stock or water

¾ cup (150 g) brown sugar

2 tbsp (30 ml) molasses

2 dried bay leaves

2 tbsp (30 ml) Worcestershire sauce

Preheat the oven to 325°F (163°C).

Brush the roast with 2 tablespoons (30 ml) of the oil and season generously with 2 tablespoons (30 g) of the salt and the pepper. In a large heavy-bottomed or cast iron stockpot over high heat, sear the meat on all sides until browned, about 3 to 4 minutes on each side. Remove and set aside. Turn down the heat to medium and let the pan cool for 5 minutes. Add the remaining 2 tablespoons (30 ml) oil and the onion and cook until it is translucent, 5 to 7 minutes, then add the garlic and cook for 2 more minutes. Add the elderberries, vinegar, wine, stock, brown sugar, molasses, bay leaves and Worcestershire sauce. Bring this mixture to a simmer and cook, with the pot's lid slightly ajar, for 1 hour.

Remove the bay leaves and the onion. Discard the bay leaves, but reserve the onion. When the liquid is cool enough to handle, strain the liquid into another large, ovenproof pot (with a lid that can also go into the oven). Empty the berries and the liquid into a medium food mill and process over a large bowl until all you have left are seeds in the mill. Discard the seeds. Return the elderberry liquid to the pot.

Transfer the roast back into the elderberry puree liquid and stir. Position in the center rack of the oven and cook, covered, for 2 hours. Uncover and cook for another 30 to 40 minutes. Check the meat. It should be falling off the bones and very tender. Carefully transfer the roast to a platter.

On the stovetop, bring the pot of the liquid to a simmer over medium-high heat and reduce by half, about 7 to 10 minutes. Do not salt until it's finished reducing. It should thicken and coat the back of a spoon. Taste for salt and add the remaining 1 teaspoon salt if needed.

Brush or pour the thickened sauce over the roast. I like to serve this with the braised onions, green beans, turnip or celery root mash and lots of cracked black pepper.

Elderflower Butter-Poached Lobster with Pickled *Elderflowers*

Lobster, Elderflower and Wine

Serves 2 — Difficulty level: Easy

This is a decadent dish, for sure, but definitely not difficult. Perfectly poached, tender, sweet lobster tails are lovely with a fragrant elderflower beurre blanc and tangy, pickled elderflowers. You can make this dish year-round by making your Elderflower Cordial and Pickled Elderflowers (see page 187 and 193, respectively). This would be an amazing New Year's Eves dish. The only trick is to have really cold butter for the poaching butter emulsion.

4 (4-oz [113-g]) fresh or frozen lobster tails

1 tbsp (15 ml) water

½ cup (115 g) Elderflower Butter (page 193), cold, cubed

½ medium shallot, minced

1 tbsp (15 ml) Elderflower Cordial (page 187)

1 tsp elderflower wine or dry white wine

1 tsp Elderflower Vinegar (page 193) or champagne vinegar

Pinch sea salt

White pepper, to taste

Pickled Elderflowers (page 193), as needed, for garnish

Rinse the lobster tails thoroughly to remove any sand or debris. In a small pot over high heat, blanch the lobster tails in lightly salted boiling water for 2 minutes. Fish them out of the water and let them cool slightly so you can handle them. While they are still very warm, squeeze the lobster tails gently between your hands to loosen the meat from the shell. With your hands, pull the meat from the tail in one, firm motion. The lobster tail should still be raw inside. Discard the cooking water.

To a small saucepan over medium-high heat, add the water and bring it to a boil quickly. With a whisk, add a few cubes of the butter and whisk vigorously to emulsify. Bring the heat down to medium and add the shallot while whisking. Add more butter cubes, 2 to 3 at a time, while whisking continuously. When you've added about half the butter, add the cordial, wine and vinegar. Continue adding the rest of the butter. The mixture should be completely emulsified, scented with elderflower and light yellow in color. Add salt and pepper to taste.

Turn down the heat to medium-low. Add 2 of the tails and submerge them in the emulsified butter and rapidly spoon the butter over the tails for 5 to 7 minutes. Repeat this process to poach the remaining 2 lobster tails.

To assemble the dish, arrange the tails on the plate and spoon the flavored, emulsified butter over them generously. Garnish with about 1 teaspoon of pickled elderflowers for an acidic pop. This dish would be lovely served with some simply dressed butter lettuce or chickweed or some with some simply dressed butter lettuce, purslane or some duchess potatoes.

Note: If you don't want to remove the tails from the shells, your fishmonger would be happy to do this.

Elderflower Butter

Creamy Butter and Aromatic Elderflower

Makes 1 cup (455 g) — Difficulty level: Easy

There is nothing more divine than the smell of elderflower butter. I dare you to find one thing it's not good on. Melt it on pancakes, slather on sweet brioche or add to butter sauces for a magical, elderflower-infused dish.

16 tbsp (230 g) butter (about 2 sticks)

1 cup (38 g) elderflowers, stemmed

In a small pot over very low heat, melt the butter completely. This should take 10 to 15 minutes. Let the butter cool a bit. While the butter is still very warm to the touch but not hot, pack in the elderflowers. Put the lid on the jar and let it cool all the way. Steep the flowers in the butter for 3 to 4 days in the fridge. Take the butter out of the fridge and submerge it in a bowl of warm water and gently melt the butter. Line a large strainer with a double layer of cheesecloth. Pour the butter through the strainer into an airtight container with a tight-fitting lid that holds at least 2 cups (480 ml), such as a mason jar. Wring any excess butter from the cheesecloth and discard the flowers. Store the clarified elderflower butter in the fridge for up to 2 weeks.

Pickled Elderflowers and Elderflower Vinegar

In chapter 2, there is a simple recipe for Chervil Vinegar on page 25. Here, you'll follow the same instructions to make elderflower vinegar, using the little florets picked off the umbels (or heads) along with any pollen. The by-product of elderflower vinegar are the pickled flowers, which are a beautiful, fragrant condiment wherever a dish needs brightening.

Elderflower Sangria with Summer Fruit

Elderflower Cordial-Infused Wine, Peach Brandy and Stone Fruits

Serves: 4-6 — Difficulty level: Easy

I love dry, mineral-tasting wines like Vinho Verde or cava. They are relatively inexpensive and widely available. Now that you have made elderflower cordial and vinegar, you're set to make a sangria, of sorts. This cocktail is a cross between a shrub and a sangria and takes advantage of the gorgeous summer stone fruits. If you make this in colder months, it pairs well with apples and pears, as well.

1 (26-oz [750-ml]) bottle sparkling dry Spanish cava or Vinho Verde

1 cup (240 ml) Elderflower Cordial (page 187)

2 tbsp (30 ml) Elderflower Vinegar (page 193)

2 medium peaches, cored and sliced

2 medium nectarines, cored and sliced

¼ cup (60 ml) peach brandy, optional

Add the cava, cordial, vinegar, peaches, nectarines and brandy (if using) to a large glass pitcher or quart (960 ml) jar. Give it a good stir and let this sit 8 hours or up to overnight in the refrigerator. Before serving, shake over ice and pour.

Elderflower Gelato

Elderflower Cordial and Cream

Serves: 6-8 — Difficulty level: Easy

This gelato recipe is adapted from *Flavor Flours* by Alice Medrich. I love this "quick gelato" recipe because it lets the subtle flavor of the elderflower shine without the influence of egg flavor or condensed milk flavor. I also like it because it requires so few ingredients. It's dense and rich yet light and perfect for summer.

Pinch sea salt

¾ cup (144 g) sugar

2 tbsp (21 g) superfine white rice flour (see note)

2¼ cups (540 ml) heavy cream, divided

¾ cup (180 ml) Elderflower Cordial (page 187)

Prepare the ice cream machine by freezing the machine's ice cream bowl for 8 hours or up to overnight.

To a medium saucepan, add the salt, sugar and rice flour and whisk to combine. Add 2 tablespoons (30 ml) of the cream and whisk to make an even paste. Over medium-low heat, start whisking in the rest of the cream and cook, stirring, for 3 to 5 minutes, until the mixture bubbles a little and it thickens a bit. Off the heat, whisk the cordial in and combine well.

Pour the mixture into a bowl and cover it with plastic wrap so the mixture doesn't form a skin. Let this chill in the refrigerator for 8 hours or up to overnight. Pour the chilled mixture into the frozen ice cream bowl and let the mixture churn for 18 to 20 minutes or according to the manufacturer's instructions. Transfer the gelato to a freezer-proof container and let it chill for at least 4 hours.

Serve the gelato with Cattail Pollen Madeleines (page 67) or spoon it into gluten-free meringues.

Note: Regular rice flour is typically made by grinding medium- or long-grain rice into a powder. Superfine rice flour is made by grinding short-grain and/or sticky glutinous rice into a finer powder. This produces a flour with a higher starch content that will dissolve much easier, making it ideal for thickening liquids.

Elderflower Cordial Tres Leches Cake

Sponge Cake Soaked in Elderberry-Infused Milk and Cream

Serves: 6-8 — Difficulty Level: Easy

This is my favorite cake and dessert in the world. It's not something I make or eat often. Although it's rich and decadent, it's a surprisingly light dessert that's great during warm months, as it's chilled. What makes this cake special is the addition of elderflower butter and infused cream. The creamy, neutral cake is a blank slate for the subtlety of the elderflowers. A *tres leches* cake is a light sponge cake with several types of milks (condensed, evaporated, whole milk and cream) that soak into the cake and almost transform it into a pudding. This is an easy dish and is made in three parts: the cake, the pouring liquid and the topping. You can also use a hand blender to make the entire dish.

1¾ cups (219 g) all-purpose flour

1 tsp baking powder

Pinch sea salt

5 large eggs, divided

½ cup (96 g) sugar

½ cup (120 ml) plus 3 tbsp (45 ml) Elderflower Cordial (page 187), divided

6 tbsp (84 g) Elderflower Butter (page 193), melted

1¾ cups (420 ml) heavy cream, divided

1 (12-oz [354-ml]) can evaporated milk

1 (14-oz [414-ml]) can sweetened condensed cream

¼ cup (60 ml) whole milk

1 tsp powdered sugar

Preheat the oven to 325°F (163°C).

Line the bottom of a 9 x 13–inch (23 x 33–cm) baking pan or a 9-inch (23-cm) spring form pan with parchment. Brush or spray the sides and lined bottom with oil or butter.

In a medium bowl, sift together the flour, baking powder and salt until well combined. Set aside.

In a large bowl, using a hand mixer, beat 1 of the eggs, the sugar and ½ cup (120 ml) of the cordial until frothy, about 3 to 4 minutes. Beat the remaining 4 eggs in, one at a time, until smooth and light yellow. Continue beating and drizzle in the butter until well incorporated, about 1 minute. Gently fold in the flour mixture until just incorporated, taking care not to overmix as the cake will be dense. Pour the batter into the prepared pan and bake on the middle rack for 30 to 35 minutes or until slightly browned on the top. Test the cake. A toothpick or butter knife should come out clean.

While the cake is baking, prepare the pouring liquid. (You'll want to pour this over the cake while it's still warm or the cake won't absorb the liquid.) In a small pot over medium-low heat, combine 1 cup (240 ml) of the cream, the evaporated milk, condensed milk and whole milk and heat, stirring, until very warm to the touch, about 4 to 5 minutes. Take the pot off the heat and, just before you pour the liquid over the cake, whisk in 2 tablespoons (30 ml) of the cordial.

Remove the cake from the oven and place it on a cool baking sheet to collect any spillover. Poke holes in the cake, going all the way to the bottom with a rounded bamboo skewer. Slowly pour the warm milk and cream mixture over the entire cake (about ½ cup [120 ml] at a time), making sure it absorbs completely before pouring more. Let the cake cool to room temperature, cover with plastic wrap and refrigerate for 8 hours or up to overnight.

Before serving, in a medium bowl and using a hand mixer, beat the remaining ¾ cup (180 ml) cream, the remaining 1 tablespoon (15 ml) cordial and powdered sugar into soft peaks, 6 to 7 minutes, and spoon over the cake. Served chilled with some coffee.

Elderberry Corn Cake

Blue Cornmeal, Elderberries and Currants

Serves: 6-8 — Difficulty level: Easy

This recipe is loosely based on a Native American Diné ceremonial *kinaalda* cake. A kinaalda is a maturity ceremony central to the Diné culture. It's an interesting texture, both moist and dense and not too sweet. The complexity of flavor comes from the almost smoky, tannic quality of the dried berries. I find this cake comforting and addictive at the same time. It gets its deep purple color from reconstituted dried elderberries and blue cornmeal. This is an extremely easy recipe, but takes quite of bit of time (about five hours). This is an excellent project for both kids and adults alike.

Vegetable oil, as needed

6½ cups (1.6 L) water

3 cups (270 g) dried elderberries

1 cup (240 ml) maple syrup or honey

6 cups (726 g) finely ground blue cornmeal (you can also use white or yellow cornmeal)

1 cup (151 g) dried currants

Pinch sea salt

Preheat the oven to 250°F (121°C).

Prepare a 9 x 13-inch (23 x 33-cm) baking dish by greasing the bottom and sides with oil.

In a medium stockpot over high heat, bring the water and dried elderberries to a boil. Lower the heat to medium-low and simmer, partially covered, for 1 hour. When the stockpot is cool enough to handle, strain the liquid into a large heat-proof bowl with a sieve. Pour the liquid back into the stockpot and, using a medium food mill, mill the elderberries over the pot until you have just seeds, scraping the pulp from the bottom of the mill. You can also do this by scraping the seeds through the sieve with the back of a wooden spoon, but it will take longer.

Stir the maple syrup or honey into the elderberry liquid to combine. Raise the heat to medium-high, bring the liquid up to a simmer, then turn off the heat. Slowly pour in the cornmeal, salt and currants, whisking constantly for 2 to 3 minutes. It will begin to thicken up almost immediately. Stir until it's a porridge-like consistency, about 3 to 4 minutes. If the mixture is too thick, add ⅛ cup (30 ml) water at a time to loosen it enough to pour. (Some corn flours absorb more liquid than others do.) Pour the mixture into the prepared baking dish and cover it tightly with aluminum foil. Bake for 4 hours.

When the corn cake has cooled, you can turn the cake out of the baking dish or just slice it out of the dish. It's wonderful with a drizzle of maple or honey. It's also great toasted on a cast iron grill with butter and elderberry jam. Store any leftovers in the refrigerator in an airtight container for up to 5 days.

Chapter Nine

Acorns and Pines

Nutty, Meaty Goodness and Fragrant Evergreen Essence

When the oak is felled the whole forest echoes with it fall, but a hundred acorns are sown in silence by an unnoticed breeze.

– Thomas Carlyle

Every string of nature's breezy harp is touched to answer thy sighs. The green oak and cedar—the dark pine, the yellow and silvery-barked willow—each majestic old tree; hath its own peculiar tone and whisper for thine ear.

– Elizabeth J. Eames, "An Autumn Reverie"

Pine

Pinus spp.

Pinaceae family

Almost all pines are fine for consumption
in small amounts for smoking foods,
teas and infusions, salts and sugars.
Note: Pregnant women should
generally avoid.

Aleppo pine (*Pinus halepensis*)

Note: I also use white fir (*Albies concolor*) quite a bit and interchangebly with pine. Fir is not a pine but it is in the Pinaceae family.

Flavor Profile

At different times of the year, the needles have a citrusy resin quality ranging from lemon to grapefruit to almost tangerine. The needles, tips and pollen can be utilized. The flavor will depend on the type of pine and the season. Chew on the needles to get the flavor profile. My favorites are white fir and pinyon pine. Some pines will never taste like anything.

White fir (*Albies concolor*)

When and How to Harvest

Pine needles can be harvested all year-round, while the pollen can be gathered in the early summer. You'll find the best pines to harvest in the mountains, where it's cooler and more temperate. Pluck the needles directly from the tree.

Distinguishing Identifiers

- Needle-like leaves arranged in a spiral around the stem that attach to a scaly sheath

- Most pine species have two to five needles per sheath and some up to eight

- Each year, trees produce a new set or "whorl" of leaves that last up to two years

- Most pines are also evergreen

- White fir has shorter needles spreading almost at right angles in two rows and the needles are a light bluish green

Possible Look-Alikes

- **Yew** (toxic)

- Australian pine (not a true pine)

- White fir can be mistaken for hemlock tree (*Tsuga* spp.). Not the same species as poison hemlock (coinum maculatum).

Acorn

Quercus spp.

Fagaceae family (oak tree in
the beech family)

You may find white, red, black, coastal
live oak and scrub oak in your area;
the acorns of each are different
in shape and flavor

Immature green acorns.

Flavor Profile

Each acorn batch is slightly different in flavor and texture.
The nut itself is slightly oily, nutty and has an almost powdery
starchy consistency. There's a sweetness and meatiness
to them after leaching, so they can have savory and sweet
applications. I often use acorns as a meat substitute or in a
puree to add body and protein to a dish.

When and How to Harvest

The trick to harvesting acorns is be on the lookout when they
start dropping, usually in the early fall (but note that some
types of acorns do not yield every year). As many foragers
and nature lovers know, nature is not a supermarket—it's
hyper-seasonal with short windows to gather and collect
before a heavy rain fells the acorns and they rot.

Shelling the Acorns

There are as many ways to do this as there are foragers. A
friend uses a heavy pipe and smashes them. Effective, if not
a little messy. I prefer to use a heavy chef's knife and place a
lightly damp towel (to prevent slippage while cutting) on a
secured cutting board. I then cut the acorn in quarters—first
horizontally, then vertically. A sharp knife and sturdy hand are
necessary.

After they are properly leached, you can dry them and grind
them for flours, roast or parch them, simmer them and use
them as a meat substitute or pickle and preserve them in
brine or syrup. We even freeze them for future use.

Acorn (Oak) Range

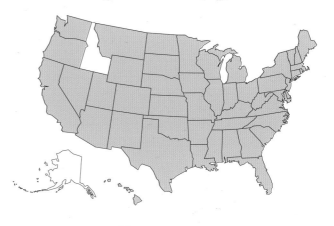

Current Known Range

Leaching acorns using a hot water process.

Hulled and leached acorns, ready for use.

Leaching the Acorns

After gathering the acorns, they must be sorted and those that are cracked or have been compromised by a worm (look for any cracks or little holes) can be discarded or returned to the ground. Those that remain are hulled and the nuts must be leached with either a cold-water or hot-water process. Here, I used a hot-water process by boiling the shelled acorns for short periods of time (20 to 30 minutes), with water changes in between extract the tannins. Note that you must change the water with hot water, not cold water. If you do so, you bind the tannins to the starch and you won't be able to get rid of the bitterness.

You'll notice the water turns a dark brown color. That is the tannins being extracted. The oak variety in our area usually takes three changes of water using the hot-water process. You need to taste them for bitterness after each leaching. Time consuming, yes. However, definitely worth the effort.

Note Boiling the acorns will cook the starch. There are reasons for cold leaching and hot leaching acorns. For the purposes of the book, I mainly use hot leaching.

Distinguishing identifiers

— The acorns of each type of oak tree can be different in shape, color and flavor; in general, the base of the acorns are usually globous, rounded, pointy or elongated and form a tapered point

— In North America and Europe, acorns have scaly "caps" that overlap in spiraling scales

— The bases of the acorns are green and gradually get darker as they mature and get larger

Possible Look-Alikes

— There are no tree nuts that resemble or would grow around oaks, to my knowledge

Acorn Sliders

Heart Veggie Burgers with Acorns and Eggplant

Serves 4-6 — Difficulty Level: Advanced

When used in savory applications, acorn has a satisfying, meaty quality that's somehow heartier than nuts. This is one my oldest recipes. Feel free to change it up or experiment with textures. Hopefully you'll be inspired to make this and also propagate acorns to plant fruit-bearing oaks on your own property.

Olive oil, as needed

1 small carrot, finely chopped

1 medium celery stalk, finely chopped

1 tsp wild fennel seeds, toasted and crushed

1 dried bay leaf

2 cloves garlic, minced

1 medium Italian eggplant, cut into ½-inch (13-mm) cubes

½ medium onion, finely chopped

¼ tsp sea salt, plus more to taste, divided

Freshly ground black pepper, to taste

1 tsp dried thyme

1 tbsp (5 g) fresh thyme

3 cups (720 ml) chicken or vegetable stock

2 cups (240 g) leached acorns, roughly chopped

½ cup (120 ml) white wine

4 oz (113 g) cooked rice noodles (al dente), roughly chopped

¼ cup (24 g) oat bran

1 large egg, beaten

¼ cup (25 g) grated Parmesan

Butter, as needed

Coat the bottom of a large heavy-bottomed sauté pan with the oil and heat it over medium heat. Add the carrot, celery, fennel seeds and bay leaf and cook for 5 to 7 minutes. Add the garlic and cook 1 more minute. You just want the vegetables a little translucent but not caramelized. Transfer the vegetables to a medium bowl and set aside to cool.

Return the sauté pan to medium-low heat and add some more oil. Once the oil is hot, cook the eggplant and onion with ¼ teaspoon salt, pepper and thyme until all the moisture is gone and it caramelizes completely, about 20 to 25 minutes.

In a small stockpot over high heat, combine the chicken stock, acorns, wine and salt. Bring to a boil, then reduce the heat to low and simmer gently for 30 minutes. Once the stockpot has cooled, strain the acorns and reserve the cooking liquid.

In a large bowl, combine the drained acorns, carrot mixture, caramelized eggplant and onion and rice noodles. Sprinkle the oat bran and acorn cooking liquid over the mixture, 1 tablespoon of each at a time, until it has the texture of stiff cookie dough. Let this cool. Note: Save your reserved liquid if you have any left. It's an excellent soup starter.

Process the cooled mixture through a hand-crank sausage grinder at a medium-coarse setting. In a large bowl, combine the ground mixture with the egg and Parmesan and incorporate well.

Form the mixture into 2- to 3-ounce (57- to 85-g) balls and chill them in the refrigerator, covered, for at least 1 hour. Preheat the oven to 350°F (177°C) and line a medium baking sheet with parchment paper.

Form the balls into little slider patties. Heat some oil and butter in a small cast iron pan over medium-high heat. Add the sliders and pan-fry the tops, bottoms and sides for 2 to 3 minutes. Bake them in the oven for 10 minutes. Serve warm.

*See image on page 202.

Acorn Miso and Maple Potatoes

Potatoes Cooked in Acorn Miso and Maple Syrup

Serves: 4 — Difficulty level: Easy

I can't tell you how much I love eating this. It reminds me that the simplest foods are some of the most beloved. This recipe serves double duty. I use this basic recipe often as a drizzle sauce on fried chicken or as a glaze for carrots or other vegetables. It's truly delicious. The following recipe is very rich but very humble at the same time. You can make this with yams, carrots or sweet potatoes as a holiday dish, but with plain old russets, it's soul-satisfying.

4 medium russet potatoes, peeled and cut into 1-inch (3-cm) cubes

1½ tbsp (17 g) Acorn Miso (page 210) or soybean miso

¼ cup (60 ml) water

1 cup (240 ml) maple syrup

4 tbsp (56 g) butter

In a medium stockpot over medium-high heat, boil the potatoes in lightly salted water for 6 to 8 minutes or until tender but a bit underdone. Check them at 6 minutes. While the potatoes are cooking, in a small bowl, whisk the miso and water together until thoroughly combined. To a small saucepan over medium heat, add the maple syrup, butter and miso water, whisking to combine. Bring the mixture just up to a bubble and bring down the heat to medium-low and let the mixture reduce slightly, 5 to 7 minutes. Add the potatoes and cook for another 3 to 4 minutes. Turn off the heat and let everything cool down together.

The hot caramel-like liquid will penetrate the potatoes. The blandness of the potatoes with the full flavor of the maple and miso are almost a shock, but in a good way. These potatoes go with practically anything, but I like them just as they are.

Note: I have made this with apples, and it's equally fabulous as a sweet and savory apple pie.

Acorn Miso

Acorns, Salt and Koji

Makes: about 8 cups (2 kg) — **Difficulty level:** Moderate

I had always wanted to make acorn miso, not only because cooked acorns remind me a little of the texture of soybeans but also because they are so nutty and protein-rich—and because I use miso pretty much on a daily basis. There are a few groups online who have suceeded beautifully, and I decided to adapt it from a straightforward miso recipe and see what happens. The act of making miso itself is quite easy if all the conditions like temperature and bacteria levels can be somewhat controlled. The process is basically mixing equal parts acorns and *kome koji* (malted rice that has been molded with koji seeds) with pure, course sea salt and fermenting it. It takes anywhere from six to twelve months to ferment and mature into a nutty, savory, umami paste. I started in early winter and luckily for me, we had a warm winter and it developed fairly quickly.

8 cups (960 g) acorns, leached and skins rubbed off

4 oz (115 g) coarse sea salt (such as French sel gris), plus more as needed

8 cups (1.8 kg) koji, crumbled and broken apart

In a medium stockpot over high heat, cover the acorns with 1 inch (3 cm) water, bring them to a boil and cook for 20 minutes. Reserve 1 cup (240 ml) of the cooking liquid. You want the acorns to be slightly warm and a little softer before you grind them. In a large bowl, combine the salt and koji and mix well. Set aside. Once the acorns are a little cooler, set a sausage grinder to the finest setting. Run the acorns through the grinder and combine them with the koji-salt mixture in the bowl and really work it with your hands. Drizzle in the reserved cooking liquid until the mixture forms a tight, well-combined paste. You may not quite use up all the liquid.

Have a sanitized, food-safe, 4-cup (960-ml) container with a tight-fitting lid ready. Roll the acorn mixture into 2-inch (5-cm) balls and start to layer them evenly at the bottom of the bucket. Pat them down to avoid any air pocket that might introduce bacteria.

Wrap a heavy plate roughly the size of the bucket with plastic wrap. Use it as a weight to push the mixture down evenly. Remove the plate and evenly coat the entire surface of the mixture with more salt to seal it and prevent bacteria. Place the covered weight back on top. Add two layers of clean cheesecloth or muslin over the top and secure it with twine or a string. Place this smaller bucket inside a larger one and just lay the lid loosely on top, not sealing it. Keep this in a dry, dark, cool corner of your house.

Every 3 weeks or so, scrape off the salt from the surface and mix the contents from bottom to top, bringing the bottom layer to the top. Cover again with salt, put the covered weight back on it, secure the cheesecloth and position the smaller bucket back into the larger bucket. Each time you do this, really smell it and look at it for any signs of rot. It should smell like beer and sake and have a slightly fermented, but not sour or rotting, smell. Once it has miso-like consistency, a deeper color and the pleasant nutty smell and taste you want, transfer the acorn miso to an airtight container to the refrigerator for use. It lasts up to 6 months in the refrigerator.

Acorn-Tella

Creamy Acorn and Chocolate Spread

Makes: about 2 cups (590 g) — **Difficulty level:** Easy

I make acorn butter every now and then, but I find acorn butter to be a little chalky. I like making an acorn-chocolate spread because the chocolate and cream add the needed silkiness and richness. Follow the instructions for leaching acorns on page 206. Note that a high-speed processor is best for this recipe. Acorns have an interesting texture that doesn't break down completely without hand grinding or a high-speed machine.

10 oz (280 g) semisweet dark chocolate, roughly chopped

1½ cups (180 g) leached acorns, skins rubbed off

1½ cups (360 ml) heavy cream, plus 1 tbsp (15 ml) if needed

Pinch sea salt

¼ cup (60 ml) water

½ tsp walnut oil

1 tsp dark unsweetened cocoa powder

4 tbsp (60 ml) raw honey

Make a double boiler by adding water to a small saucepan and placing a small heat-proof bowl on top. The water should not touch the bottom of the bowl. Add the chocolate to the bowl and turn the heat to low. Stir occasionally to move the chocolate around. It should melt slowly for about 10 minutes. (Note: Avoid any water droplets or water from steam or the chocolate will break. The bowl should fit the pot exactly.) When the chocolate is thoroughly melted, take the bowl off the heat and set aside.

In a medium pot over medium heat, combine the acorns, cream, salt and water. Bring to a simmer and cook for 20 minutes. Strain the acorns, reserving the liquid, and set aside. Let the cream mixture cool enough to handle in a food processor. The acorns need to still be warm when processing.

Add the acorns to the food processor along with 2 tablespoons (30 ml) of the cooking liquid and the walnut oil. Process for 2 to 3 minutes. Add the cocoa and process for 1 minute. Add the honey and process for 1 more minute. Add the warm chocolate and process until the mixture is smooth. Finally, drizzle in the warm cream mixture slowly. If the mixture is too thick, add hot cream in ½-teaspoon increments.

Serve the acorn-tella with toast or bread, with waffles or pancakes or even fresh or dried fruit. It's wonderful with dried oranges and figs. Store the spread in a mason jar or container with a tight-fitting lid in the refrigerator for 1 week.

Note: Acorns are hygroscopic and continue to absorb liquid, much like oatmeal. If you are not using this right away, you may have to warm it slightly and add more warm cream before serving to loosen.

Pine Syrup and Pine Sugar

Sweetened Pine Flavor

Makes: about 3½ cups (840 ml) Pine Syrup and 4 cups (768 g) Pine Sugar
Difficulty level: Easy

There are many ways to make a flavored or infused sugar. There are some pretty fantastical molecular gastronomy methods that are truly amazing, but for the sake of practicality and ease, we'll chose the simplest methods. As mentioned, I interchange white fir and pine frequently depending on availability.

PINE SYRUP

2 cups (383 g) sugar

1½ cups (360 ml) water

2 cups (40 g) fresh pine or fir needles

PINE SUGAR

2 cups (383 g) sugar

2 cups (40 g) dried pine or fir needles

½ cup (10 g) fresh pine or fir needles

One very effective method is to make a heavy simple syrup, which is 1½ parts sugar to 1 part water. Add the sugar and water to a small saucepan and, over very low heat, let the mixture dissolve without stirring, about 7 to 10 minutes. You can occasionally swirl the pan. Don't let this boil or simmer.

Meanwhile, with kitchen scissors, snip the pine needles into smaller pieces to release the oils. Take the pan off the heat and add the needles. Let it cool down completely and transfer it to an airtight container or mason jar and refrigerate for at least 1 week before straining the liquid and using. The syrup will keep in the refrigerator for 3 to 5 months. This is a wonderful addition to iced tea, lemonade or mixed drinks.

For the second method, you need to dry or dehydrate the needles and the ratio of needles to sugar is equal. Snip the dried needles into small pieces and grind them gradually, along with the sugar, in an espresso grinder or a coarse mortar and pestle. Transfer the sugar to an airtight container or jar and nestle the fresh needles into the ground sugar mixture and let this infuse for 1 to 2 weeks.

Note: If you have access to rock sugar, you'll be able to get a finer grind.

Pine Beignets with Pine Cream

Fluffy Doughnuts with Pine Sugar and Pine-Infused Cream Filling

Makes: 12–15 beignets — **Difficulty level:** Moderate

Beignets are a perfect vehicle to carry pine sugar and pine pastry cream, and they are a special holiday treat for me with a cup of pine tea. I used white fir because that's what I had available at the time but you can interchange the two. This is a fairly easy recipe once you have your flavored cream and sugars done, as beignets are just little yeasted, airy bread pillows.

PINE PASTRY CREAM

1 cup (240 ml) heavy cream

½ cup (120 ml) whole milk

1 cup (20 g) fresh or dried pine or white fir needles, removed from the branch and snipped into small pieces

¼ cup (31 g) all-purpose flour

¼ cup (48 g) Pine Sugar (page 213)

4 large egg yolks, beaten

Pinch sea salt

2 tbsp (30 ml) Pine Syrup (page 213)

PINE PASTRY CREAM

In a medium saucepan over medium-high heat, bring the cream and milk up to a boil and then turn off the heat. Add the pine or white fir needles. Let this steep and cool down all the way to room temperature. Strain and set aside.

In a medium bowl, sift the flour and sugar together and whisk to combine. In another small bowl, whisk together the eggs, salt and pine syrup and combine well. Add the eggs to the flour mixture while whisking. Combine well.

To the same saucepan, add the infused cream and bring it up to a slight bubble over medium heat; do not boil or simmer and turn off the heat. Temper the eggs by ladling about ½ cup (120 ml) of the hot cream-milk mixture into the flour-egg mixture while whisking. Repeat this process until most of the mixture has been incorporated. Add the entire mixture back to the saucepan and cook over medium heat for 5 to 6 minutes, or until it's thickened into a pudding-like consistency and sticks to the back of a spoon in a thick layer.

Remove the saucepan from the heat and strain the mixture in a sieve to remove any gritty pine pieces or cooked egg pieces. Transfer the cream to a small bowl or airtight container and cover the top with plastic wrap so the cream doesn't form a skin. Let it chill for at least 4 hours or up to overnight.

BEIGNETS

¾ cup (180 ml) milk, at room temperature

¼ cup (48 g) sugar

1½ tsp (5 g) instant yeast

1 large egg, beaten

½ tsp sea salt

½ cup (120 ml) evaporated milk

3½ cups (438 g) all-purpose flour, sifted, divided

2 tbsp (28 g) cold vegetable shortening or butter, divided

Grapeseed or vegetable oil, for frying

Pine Sugar (page 213), for garnish

BEIGNETS

To a food processor fitted with the dough blade, add the milk, sugar and yeast and process for 1 minute. Let it stand in the processor for 10 minutes to bloom. In a small bowl, combine the egg, salt and evaporated milk and beat until well incorporated. Add the egg mixture to the processor and process for 1 minute or until well combined. Add 1¾ cups (219 g) of the flour and 1 tablespoon (14 g) of the shortening, pulsing only until it just comes together and the shortening distributes into small pieces. Add the remaining 1¾ cups (219 g) flour and 1 tablespoon (14 g) shortening. Don't overmix the dough.

Transfer the dough to a large oiled bowl and shape the dough into a disc or ball. Cover the bowl with oiled plastic wrap and refrigerate the dough for 8 hours or up to overnight.

The next day, fill your mini fryer with a high heat oil (like sunflower or grapeseed) according to the machine's specifications and preheat to 375°F (191°C) or you can use a cast iron pan filled with 2 inches (6 cm) of oil. While the oil is heating, remove the dough from the refrigerator and let it come to room temperature (about 10 minutes). With a floured rolling pin on a floured surface, roll the dough out to ¼-inch (6-mm) or ½-inch (13-mm) thickness. Use a circular 2-inch (6-cm) pastry cutter to punch out holes of dough (or you can simply cut 2-inch [6-cm] squares or diamonds). When the oil is ready, lightly drop the dough pieces in without crowding the mini fryer. They should start to float after about 10 seconds. Remove them when browned and place on a large paper towel–lined baking sheet or plate to drain.

When the beignets have cooled down, pipe in about 1 teaspoon of the pine cream mixture using a pastry bag with a tip and dust them with the pine or fir sugar. Enjoy right away.

Pine-Smoked Mussels with Pine Mignonette

Mussels Smoked with Pine and Dressed in Pine-Infused Vinaigrette

Serves 4-6 — Difficulty Level: Easy

This dish is one of my all-time favorite campfire dishes. It's easy, a little different fom your usual camping fare and the smell and flavors will etch themselves in your brain forever. The brininess of the mussels and the woody and resinous essence of the smoke and vinaigrette are harmonious. This is also an elegant starter and crowd pleaser.

4½ cups (90 g) fresh pine needles (or dry needles that have been soaked in water for a few minutes), divided

1 cup (240 ml) rice wine vinegar or other light vinegar

3 tbsp (45 ml) olive oil

1 tsp freshly cracked pink or green peppercorns

½ tsp honey

3 cups (60 g) dried pine or fir needles, divided

2 lb (910 g) fresh mussels, cleaned and scrubbed

2 medium shallots, minced

Sea salt, to taste

To make the mignonette, wash and dry ½ cup (10 g) of the fresh pine needles. Remove them from the stem and, with a really sharp knife, mince them very finely and set aside. In a small bowl, combine the vinegar, oil, peppercorns, honey and the minced needles and stir to thoroughly combine. Let this marinate for at least 2 hours (overnight is ideal).

Soak 1½ cups (30 g) of the dried pine needles in water for 5 minutes and drain. Place the remaining 1½ cups (30 g) dried pine needles on a large perforated sheet pan (or you can use 3 to 4 layers of heavy aluminum foil and poke holes in it) and place it directly on the grill. Close the grill top for 5 minutes. The needles with singe and smoke. Carefully scatter the mussels on top of the smoking needles and cover with fresh pine needles (or soaked dry needles) and close the grill. Cook for 5 to 7 minutes or until all the mussels open. Discard any mussels that do not open. The mussels will have a subtle, smoky, pine-infused flavor.

Spoon the mignonette generously over the cooked mussels and serve.

Resources

Books

Botany in a Day: The Patterns Method of Plant Identification by Thomas J. Elpel

Native American Ethnobotany by Daniel Moerman

Guide to Wild Foods and Useful Plants by Christopher Nyerges

Foraging Wild Edible Plants of North America: More Than 150 Delicious Recipes Using Nature's Edibles by Christopher Nyerges

The New Wildcrafted Cuisine: Exploring the Exotic Gastronomy of Local Terroir by Pascal Baudar

Backyard Foraging: 65 Plants You Didn't Know You Could Eat by Ellen Zachos

The Forager's Feast: How to Identify, Gather, and Prepare Wild Edibles by Leda Meredith

Preserving Everything: Can, Culture, Pickle, Freeze, Ferment, Dehydrate, Salt, Smoke, and Store Fruits, Vegetables, Meat, Milk, and More by Leda Meredith

The Locavore's Handbook: The Busy Person's Guide To Eating Local on a Budget by Leda Meredith

Idiot's Guides: Foraging by Mark "Merriweather" Vorderbruggen, PhD

Free Food from Foraging by Karen Stephenson

Hunt, Gather, Cook: Finding the Forgotten Feast by Hank Shaw

Southeast Foraging: 120 Wild and Flavorful Edibles from Angelica to Wild Plums by Chris Bennett

Edible Wild Plants: A North American Field Guide to over 200 Natural Foods by Thomas Elias and Peter Dykeman

Pacific Northwest Foraging: 112 Wild and Flavorful Edibles from Alaska Blueberries to Wild Hazelnuts by Douglas Deur

Foraging the Rocky Mountains: Finding, Identifying, and Preparing Edible Wild Foods in the Rockies by Liz Brown Morgan

Midwest Foraging: 115 Wild and Flavorful Edibles from Burdock to Wild Peach by Lisa M. Rose

Mountain States Foraging: 115 Wild and Flavorful Edibles from Alpine Sorrel to Wild Hops by Briana Wiles

Southwest Foraging: 117 Wild and Flavorful Edibles from Barrel Cactus to Wild Oregano by John Slattery

Edible Wild Plants: Wild Foods from Dirt to Plate by John Kallas

Nature's Garden: A Guide to Identifying, Harvesting, and Preparing Edible Wild Plants by Samuel Thayer

The Joy of Foraging: Gary Lincoff's Illustrated Guide to Finding, Harvesting, and Enjoying a World of Wild Food by Gary Lincoff

Wild Food Plants of Hawai'i by Sunny Savage

Wild Plants I Have Known . . . and Eaten by Russ Cohen

The Wild Wisdom of Weeds: 13 Essential Plants for Human Survival by Katrina Blair

Eat Your Drink: Culinary Cocktails by Matthew Biancaniello

66 Square Feet: A Delicious Life by Marie Viljoen

Eating Wildly: Foraging for Life, Love and the Perfect Meal by Ava Chin

Noted Researchers, Authors and Scholars

Rosalee de la Foret

Holly Drake

David Spahr

Kiva Rose

Mackenzie Burton Sanders

Online Resources

United States Department of Agriculture (http://plants.usda.gov)

E-Flora BC (http://ibis.geog.ubc.ca/biodiversity/eflora)

SELF NutritionData (http://nutritiondata.self.com)

Invasive Plant Atlas of the United States (http://www.invasiveplantatlas.org)

Friends of the Wild Flower Garden (http://www.friendsofthewildflowergarden.org)

Dr. Andrew Weil, MD (http://www.drweil.com)

Eat That Weed (http://www.eatthatweed.com)

Utah State University Extension (https://extension.usu.edu/weedguides/)

The Permaculture Project (http://www.permacultureproject.com)

eFlora (http://www.efloras.org)

Wildflowers and Weeds (http://www.wildflowers-and-weeds.com)

Garden Guides (http://www.gardenguides.com)

Eat the Weeds (http://eattheweeds.com)

Edible Wild Food (http://www.ediblewildfood.com)

Native Tech (http://www.nativetech.org)

Navajo People (http://navajopeople.org/)

Return to Nature (http://returntonature.us/)

Homestead.org (http://homestead.org/)

Gardening Know How (http://www.gardeningknowhow.com/)

Plants for a Future (http://www.pfaf.org/)

Temperate Climate Permaculture (http://tcpermaculture.blogspot.com/)

Botanical.com (http://www.botanical.com/)

The Jepson Herbarium (http://ucjeps.berkeley.edu/eflora/)

Wolf Camp and the Conservation College (http://www.wolfcollege.com/)

Acknowledgments

Biggest thanks to Marissa Giambelluca and William Kiester at Page Street Publishing for believing in *Ugly Little Greens*! Thank you to Nichole Kraft for her eagle-eye copyediting and patience. Special thanks to Pascal Baudar, Abbe Findley, Sara Griffith, Melissa Brown Bidermann and Sergio Perera for the love and support. Thank you to Opinel, Angeles Crest Creamery, Harmony Farms, Fish King, Stephanie Mutz at Sea Stephanie Fish, Altadena Farmers Market and Santa Monica Farmers Market for your wonderful products and excellent customer service.

About the Author

Mia Wasilevich is a chef, forager, wildcrafter, artist, food photographer, educator and founder of Transitional Gastronomy, which is based in Los Angeles, California. She creates pop-ups and events featuring local forages. She also teaches wild-food identification, food styling and culinary workshops. Her nature-based cuisine is influenced by the more than twenty countries she'd traveled to before the age of fifteen. An avid researcher, Mia aims to uncover forgotten foods and re-create them for the modern palate. She has been a featured consultant on *MasterChef* and *Top Chef*. She has been in *Los Angeles* magazine's "2015 Best of LA: Favorite Things" list as well as numerous other publications, including *Time* magazine, the *Los Angeles Times*, and Tastemade. Mia considers herself "a little bit country and a little bit escargot." Follow Mia at transitionalgastronomy.com.

Index